W9-CCN-584

ERICA ★ THE ★ BEAUTIFUL

How to Use This Book

Look for these special features in this book:

SIDEBARS, **CHARTS**, **GRAPHS**, and original **MAPS** expand your understanding of what's being discussed—and also make useful sources for classroom reports.

FAQs answer common **F**requently **A**sked **Q**uestions about people, places, and things.

WOW FACTORS offer "Who knew?" facts to keep you thinking.

TRAVEL GUIDE gives you tips on exploring the state—either in person or right from your chair!

PROJECT ROOM provides fun ideas for school assignments and incredible research projects. Plus, there's a guide to primary sources—what they are and how to cite them.

Please note: All statistics are as up-to-date as possible at the time of publication.

Consultants: William Loren Katz; Kimberly K. Porter, Professor of History, University of North Dakota; Donald P. Schwert, Professor of Geology, North Dakota State University

Book production by The Design Lab

Library of Congress Cataloging-in-Publication Data
Stille, Darlene R.
 North Dakota / by Darlene R. Stille.
    p. cm.—(America the beautiful. Third series)
 Includes bibliographical references and index.
 ISBN-13: 978-0-531-18502-5
 ISBN-10: 0-531-18502-8
 1. North Dakota—Juvenile literature. I. Title. II. Series.
 F651.3.S75 2010
 978.4—dc22   2008011282

No part of this publication may be reproduced in whole or in part, or stored in a retrieval system, or transmitted in any form or by any means, electronic, mechanical, photocopying, recording, or otherwise, without written permission of the publisher. For information regarding permission, write to Scholastic Inc., 557 Broadway, New York, NY 10012.

©2010 Scholastic Inc.
All rights reserved. Published in 2010 by Children's Press, an imprint of Scholastic Inc.
Published simultaneously in Canada. Printed in the United States of America.
SCHOLASTIC, CHILDREN'S PRESS, and associated logos are trademarks and/or registered trademarks of Scholastic Inc.

1 2 3 4 5 6 7 8 9 10 R 19 18 17 16 15 14 13 12 11 10

North Dakota

BY DARLENE R. STILLE

Third Series

Children's Press®
An Imprint of Scholastic Inc.
New York ★ Toronto ★ London ★ Auckland ★ Sydney
Mexico City ★ New Delhi ★ Hong Kong
Danbury, Connecticut

CONTENTS

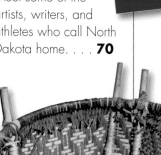

GROWTH AND CHANGE

4

Towns grow along railroad tracks, Lakotas battle to keep their land, and immigrants pour into the new state. **44**

BROADWAY, LOOKING SOUTH, FARGO, N. D.

MORE MODERN TIMES

5

Great clouds of black dust blow across the plains during the drought of the 1930s, Native American code talkers help win World War II, and oil is discovered. **56**

9 TRAVEL GUIDE

Explore North Dakota's welcoming towns, rugged landscapes, and intriguing historic sites. **104**

PROJECT ROOM

★

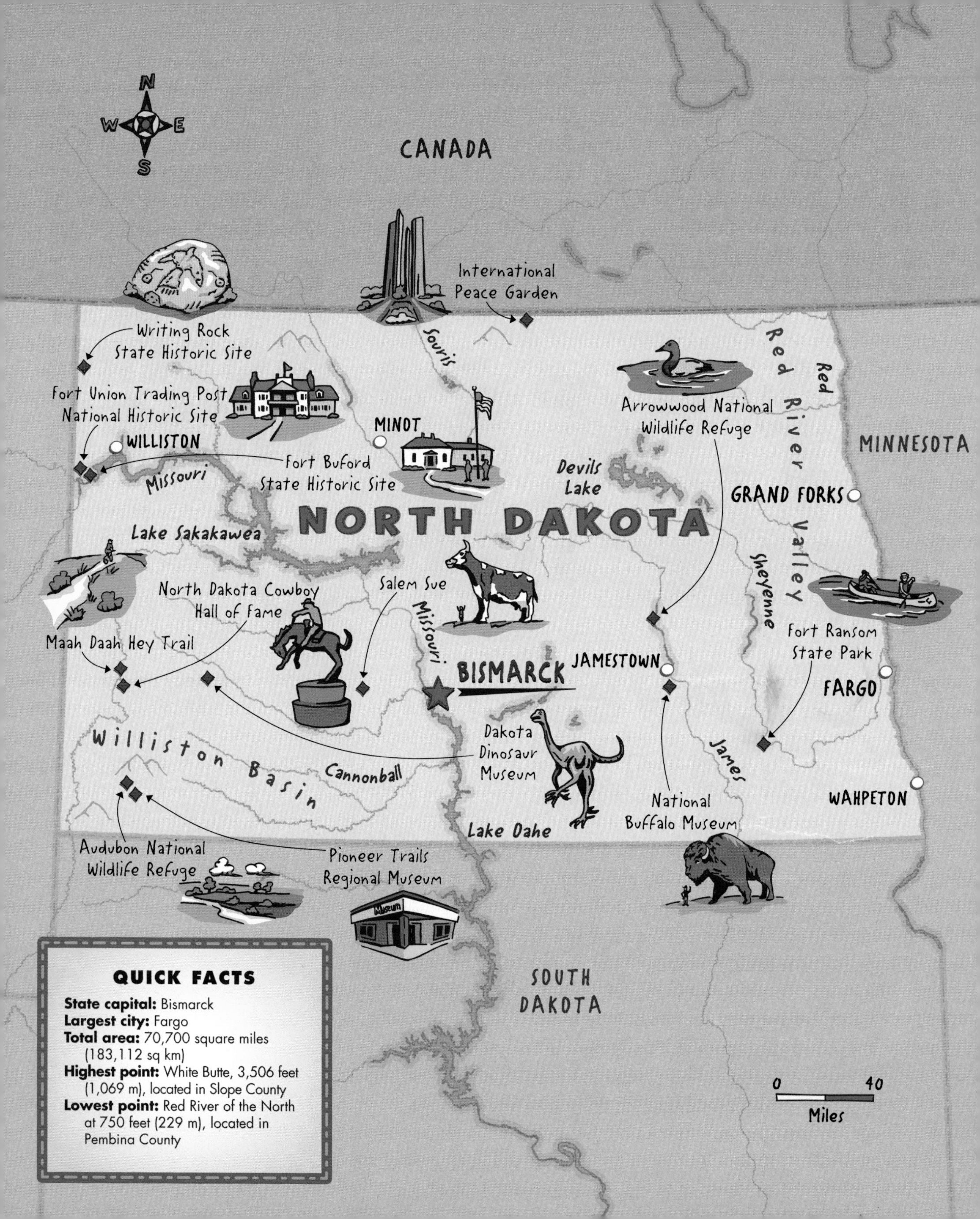

CANADA

International
Peace Garden

Writing Rock
State Historic Site

Souris

Arrowwood National
Wildlife Refuge

Red River Valley

Red

Fort Union Trading Post
National Historic Site

MINOT

MINNESOTA

WILLISTON

Fort Buford
State Historic Site

Missouri

Devils
Lake

GRAND FORKS

NORTH DAKOTA

Lake Sakakawea

Sheyenne

North Dakota Cowboy
Hall of Fame

Salem Sue

Fort Ransom
State Park

Maah Daah Hey Trail

Missouri

BISMARCK

JAMESTOWN

FARGO

Williston Basin

Cannonball

Dakota
Dinosaur
Museum

James

WAHPETON

Audubon National
Wildlife Refuge

Pioneer Trails
Regional Museum

National
Buffalo Museum

Lake Oahe

SOUTH
DAKOTA

QUICK FACTS

State capital: Bismarck
Largest city: Fargo
Total area: 70,700 square miles
(183,112 sq km)
Highest point: White Butte, 3,506 feet
(1,069 m), located in Slope County
Lowest point: Red River of the North
at 750 feet (229 m), located in
Pembina County

0   40
Miles

Welcome to North Dakota!

HOW DID NORTH DAKOTA GET ITS NAME?

In the 1700s, several groups of Native Americans lived on the northern plains, including a group that called itself the Dakota, which means "friend." The United States bought most of the land that became North Dakota in 1803, and in 1861 made it part of a new territory, which Congress named the Dakota Territory. When the territory was later divided into states, Congress named one North Dakota.

NORTH DAKOTA

MICHIGAN

MINNESOTA

WISCONSIN

8

READ ABOUT

Little bluestem
prairie grass
at Theodore
Roosevelt
National Park

CHAPTER ONE

LAND

★

WHAT ARE THE "AMBER WAVES OF GRAIN" FROM THE SONG "AMERICA THE BEAUTIFUL"? They could easily describe the golden wheat covering much of North Dakota's 70,700 square miles (183,112 square kilometers). Corn and other crops also grow in fertile valleys throughout the state. The highest point, White Butte, rises 3,506 feet (1,069 meters) above sea level in the southwestern part of the state. The lowest point is 750 feet (229 m) above sea level in the northeast along the Red River of the North.

The Red River of the North flows through fertile valleys in the state.

WORDS TO KNOW

receded *pulled or moved back over time*

sediment *material eroded from rocks and deposited elsewhere by wind, water, or glaciers*

FROM ICE AND WATER

North Dakota is a state with a hot and cold past. Farmers and miners can thank that past for the state's rich soil and abundant deposits of coal and oil.

Millions of years ago, North Dakota was at the bottom of a warm, shallow sea. The sea eventually **receded**, and in its place grew swamps where dinosaurs and other large creatures roamed. When the swamp plants died, they were buried under **sediment**, where the heat and pressure began to change them into coal. About 2 million years ago, the climate began to grow cold, and huge ice sheets called glaciers slowly advanced south from the Arctic. When the climate warmed again, the glaciers receded to the frozen north. The glaciers advanced and receded several times during this period, which is called the ice age. As they moved, the glaciers ground up rocks and flattened the surface. The last glacier receded from North Dakota about 10,000 years ago.

Before the ice age, the Missouri River flowed northward, but the advance of glaciers forced it to seek a southward route. The present path of the Missouri River approximately outlines how far south the glaciers advanced. As the glaciers moved, they created Lake Agassiz, which was filled with cold, melted ice water. The huge lake covered what became the Red River Valley. The lake water was full of fine silt and clay that had been created as the glacier ground rocks and soil to powder. The silt and clay gradually settled to the lake bottom. When the lake finally drained as the ice receded, the silt and clay that was left behind formed the basis for some of the world's finest soil.

Lake Agassiz was larger than all five of the present-day Great Lakes combined.

North Dakota Geo-Facts

Along with the state's geographical highlights, this chart ranks North Dakota's land, water, and total area compared to all other states.

Total area; rank . . . . . 70,700 square miles (183,112 sq km); 19th
Land; rank . . . . 68,976 square miles (178,647 sq km); 17th
Water; rank . . . . 1,724 square miles (4,465 sq km), 22nd
Inland water; rank . . . . . . 1,724 square miles (4,465 sq km), 12th
Geographic center . . . Sheridan, 5 miles (8 km) southwest of McClusky
Latitude . . . . 45°55' N to 49° N
Longitude . . . . 97° W to 104° W
Highest point . . . . White Butte, 3,506 feet (1,069 m), located in Slope County
Lowest point . . . . Red River of the North at 750 feet (229 m), located in Pembina County
Largest city . . . . Fargo
Longest river . . . . Red River of the North

Source: U.S. Census Bureau

Rhode Island, the smallest state, could fit inside North Dakota 46 times.

North Dakota Topography

Use the color-coded elevation chart to see on the map North Dakota's high points (dark orange) and low points (green). Elevation is measured as the distance above or below sea level.

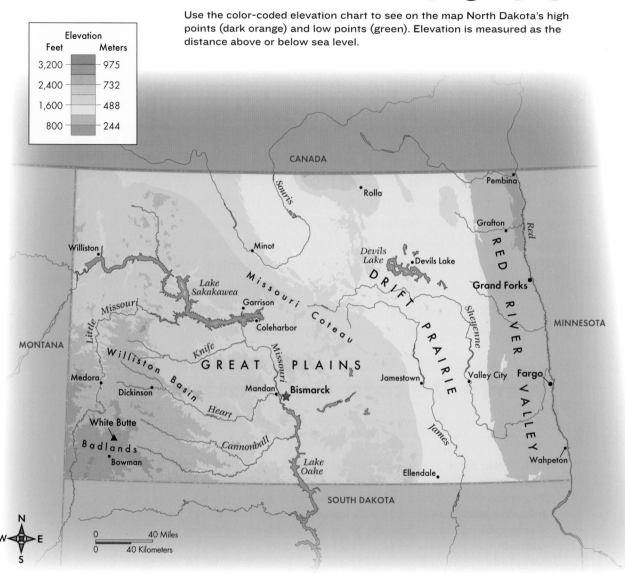

Elevation

Feet	Meters
3,200	975
2,400	732
1,600	488
800	244

LAND REGIONS

North Dakota can be divided into three land regions, which stretch westward like three huge steps. The Red River Valley is the lowest, then there is a step up to the Drift Prairie, and another step up to the Great Plains.

A canola field in McLean County

Red River Valley

This strip of fertile land spreads out about 10 to 40 miles (16 to 64 km) on either side of the Red River of the North. It runs southward from the Canadian province of Manitoba through eastern North Dakota. At an elevation of 800 to 1,000 feet (244 to 305 m), it is the lowest, flattest region of the state.

Drift Prairie

The next step up is the Drift Prairie, which rises from 1,300 to 1,600 feet (396 to 488 m) above sea level. A steep slope called an escarpment divides this region of rolling hills from the Red River Valley. The prairie is covered with soil and rocks deposited by glaciers long ago. In the north are the Pembina Hills and the Turtle Mountains.

SEE IT HERE!

THEODORE ROOSEVELT NATIONAL PARK

Named for President Theodore Roosevelt, who once owned ranches in the Badlands, this national park is a scenic area of strange rock formations. Wind and water began to erode the Badlands even before the glaciers covered the region. After the ice sheets melted, rivers and streams that ran across the land continued to carve buttes, valleys, and fantastic shapes. A soft coal called **lignite** lies under the Badlands. Occasionally, it caught fire, and the heat from the underground fires colored parts of the rock brick red. Erosion continues to shape the Badlands today.

WORD TO KNOW

lignite *a soft type of coal that does not produce as much energy as hard coal*

Great Plains

The southwestern half of North Dakota is part of the Great Plains. North Dakotans call this region the Missouri Plateau. It rises from about 2,000 feet (610 m) to more than 3,000 feet (914 m) above sea level.

The Missouri River, which flows into the Mississippi, is the main river in the western part of the state. One of the most striking features in southwestern North Dakota is an area along the Little Missouri River called the Badlands, where wind and water have eroded the landscape into fantastic shapes.

CLIMATE

Winters in North Dakota can be brutally cold. Temperatures drop below 0°F (–18°C) an average of 65 days a year near the Canadian border and 35 days a year in the southwestern part of the state. Winds gusting across the plains and prairies make the temperatures feel even colder. Summer days usually have plenty of sunshine and low humidity. Throughout much of the state, temperatures top 90°F (32°C).

Weather Report

This chart shows record temperatures (high and low) for the state, as well as average temperatures (July and January) and average annual precipitation.

Record high temperature . . . 121°F (49°C) at Steele on July 6, 1936
Record low temperature . . . . –60°F (–51°C) at Parshall
on February 15, 1936
Average July temperature .70°F (21°C)
Average January temperature . . . . .10°F (–12°C)
Average yearly precipitation . . . . .16 inches (41 cm)

Source: National Climatic Data Center, NESDIS, NOAA, U.S. Department of Commerce

Members of the U.S. Coast Guard use a boat to travel through Grand Forks after the April 1997 flood.

THE FLOOD AND FIRE OF 1997

The Red River of the North flows northward, and sometimes ice to the north blocks the warmer river water that is flowing into it. This situation contributed to one of the worst floods in North Dakota's history, which occurred in April 1997. Over the previous winter, blizzards had dumped up to 100 inches (254 cm) of snow on the region. As the snow began to melt, torrential rains poured down. The combination of snowmelt, rain, and ice blockage caused the Red River to overflow its banks at Grand Forks. Most of the city's 50,000 residents had to be evacuated. With the downtown under water, a fire broke out. Firefighters could not reach fire hydrants, which were also under water. Eleven buildings burned down, and the flood caused more than $4 billion in damage.

Western North Dakota has a **semiarid** climate. On average, it gets more rainfall than a desert, but less rainfall than farmlands in the milder Midwest. The state's average rainfall is 16 inches (41 centimeters) a year. Often, however, the state experiences droughts, times when there is much less rainfall.

North Dakota is also frequently hit by tornadoes. Between 1950 and 2004, an average of 21 tornadoes a year whirled across North Dakota, but in 1999, 65 tornadoes ripped through the state. North Dakota's deadliest tornado, which had winds of more than 300 miles per hour (483 kph), struck Fargo in June 1957, killing 10 people and injuring 103.

WORD TO KNOW

semiarid *receiving 10 to 20 inches (25 to 51 cm) of rain every year*

Sunflowers in bloom near a farm in
Barnes County

PLANT LIFE

Most of North Dakota was once covered with grasslands. Big bluestem grew on tallgrass prairies in the
northeast. Blue gamma and other shorter grasses covered the Drift Prairie and the Great Plains. Today, the
best places to see native grasses and colorful wildflowers, such as sunflowers, black-eyed Susans, coneflow-
ers, and goldenrod, are on state and national wildlife
refuges.

Forests cover only about 1 percent of the land in
North Dakota, mainly around Devils Lake and in the
Turtle Mountains and the Pembina Hills. The trees
include ash, aspen, elm, oak, and poplar. Cottonwoods
and willows grow along the Missouri River.

North Dakota National Park Areas

This map shows some of North Dakota's national parks, preserves, and other areas protected by the National Park Service.

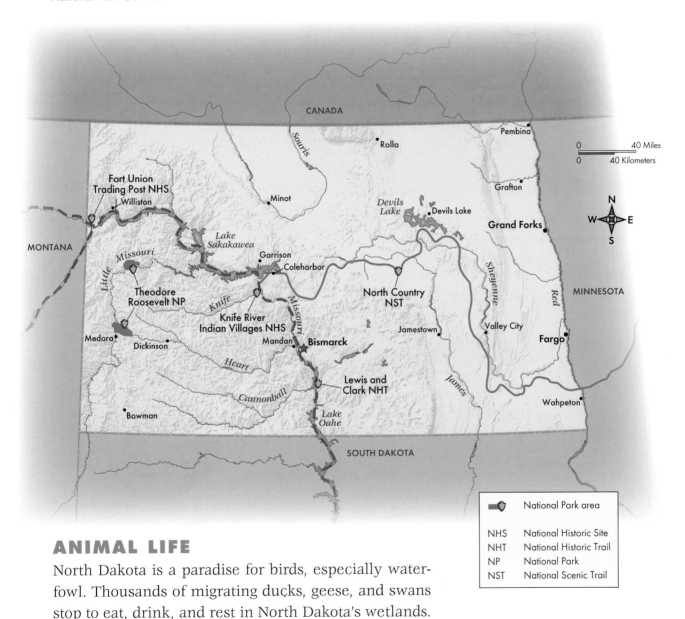

ANIMAL LIFE

North Dakota is a paradise for birds, especially water-fowl. Thousands of migrating ducks, geese, and swans stop to eat, drink, and rest in North Dakota's wetlands. Prairie potholes are part of what make North Dakota such an ideal place for migrating birds. The potholes are

BIRD BIOLOGIST

If the subject is birds, then you can be sure that biologist Katherine R. Mehl (1967–) will be interested. Born in Springfield, Missouri, she now teaches at the University of North Dakota. As part of her research, she captures and marks waterfowl and shorebirds that live near marshes, ponds, rivers, and other wetlands. This helps her keep track of the birds, so she can learn more about the health of North Dakota's birds, how many there are, how long they live, and where they travel after leaving North Dakota. By working with wildlife managers, she can help keep bird populations at healthy numbers.

An American avocet in a North Dakota marsh

depressions in the land that were formed as the ice left by receding glaciers melted. The holes filled up with water to create a series of ponds and marshes across the central part of the state.

The state's lakes and rivers teem with fish such as bass, bluegill, muskellunge, northern pike, and trout. Walleye live in the Missouri River, Devils Lake, and lakes Sakakawea and Oahe. You can catch paddlefish in the Missouri and Yellowstone rivers,

The gray wolf, once abundant in North Dakota, is now on the state's endangered species list.

ENDANGERED ANIMALS

North Dakota wildlife refuges protect **endangered** and **threatened** animals, and laws make it illegal to harm an endangered species in any way. North Dakota's endangered or threatened animals include the gray wolf and the black-footed ferret. The peregrine falcon, the piping plover, the least tern, and the whooping crane are endangered bird species, while the bald eagle is listed as threatened. The pallid sturgeon, a strange-looking fish covered with bony plates, is also endangered.

catfish in the Red River of the North, and Chinook salmon in Lake Sakakawea.

North Dakota has its share of large animals such as deer, coyotes, foxes, and mountain lions. Moose live in the Pembina Hills and other forested areas. Elk, pronghorns, and bighorn sheep live in parts of western North Dakota. The plains are also home to many small mammals such as prairie dogs, rabbits, skunks, and flicker-tail ground squirrels.

HUMANS AND THE ENVIRONMENT

North Dakota has few big cities and plenty of wide-open spaces, but pollution is still a concern. North Dakota has large deposits of soft lignite coal. Lignite contains a great deal of water and produces less energy than

WORDS TO KNOW

endangered *ar risk of becoming extinct*

threatened *likely to become endangered in the foreseeable future*

FAQ

Q8 DOES NORTH DAKOTA HAVE ANY ENDANGERED PLANTS?

A8 Yes, the western prairie fringed orchid is on the endangered plant list.

This power plant in Underwood burns lignite, a type of coal that can cause acid rain.

WORD TO KNOW

acid rain *pollution that falls to the earth in raindrops*

other types of coal. It also gives off more pollutants when it burns. North Dakota has several power plants that burn lignite, which can give off small quantities of the poisonous chemical mercury, plus other chemical compounds that combine with moisture in clouds to cause **acid rain**. In 2006, North Dakota and the U.S. Environmental Protection Agency reached an agreement to reduce pollutants that cause acid rain at two of the state's lignite-burning power plants. Researchers were also looking for cleaner ways to use lignite.

Habitat destruction has long been a concern for North Dakotans. When white settlers began to arrive in North Dakota in the 1800s, the native prairie grasses and wildflowers began to disappear. By 2000, about 99.5 percent of the original grasslands had been turned into farms and ranches. As their habitat disappeared, so did the native plants and animals that once lived there.

One of North Dakota's great environmental success stories involves the bison, which are sometimes called buffalo. Huge herds of bison once roamed the plains of North Dakota. European Americans, however, hunted the animals almost to extinction. By 1900, fewer than 600 bison remained on the Great Plains. The efforts of early conservationists such as President Theodore Roosevelt have saved the bison. Today, about 90,000 bison once again thunder across ranches and refuges in the wide-open spaces of North Dakota.

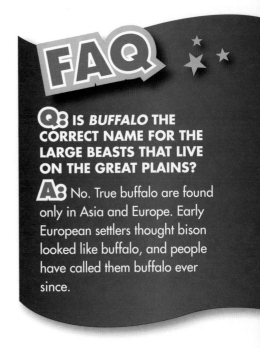

FAQ

Q8 IS _BUFFALO_ THE CORRECT NAME FOR THE LARGE BEASTS THAT LIVE ON THE GREAT PLAINS?

A8 No. True buffalo are found only in Asia and Europe. Early European settlers thought bison looked like buffalo, and people have called them buffalo ever since.

Bison grazing in Theodore Roosevelt National Park

READ ABOUT

Hunters from Asia crossed the Bering Strait during the last ice age. Their descendants eventually settled in North Dakota and other parts of North America.

Woodland bowl

c. 13,000 BCE

The first human beings arrive in what is now North Dakota

▲ c. 500 BCE

The Woodland period begins

c. 100 BCE

People in North Dakota begin trading with people to the south and the east

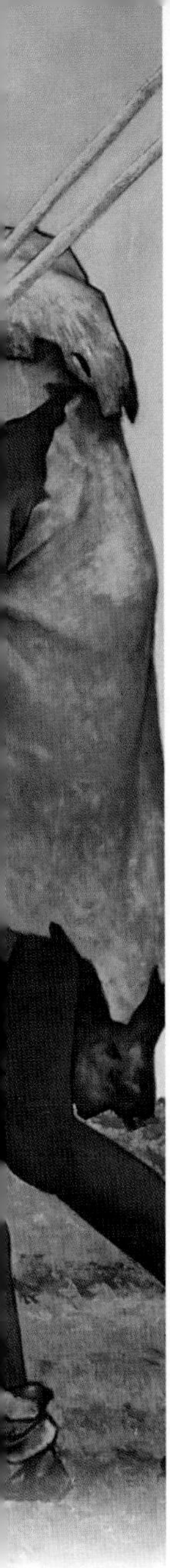

CHAPTER TWO

FIRST PEOPLE

★

MANY EXPERTS BELIEVE THAT THE ANCESTORS OF NORTH DAKOTA'S FIRST SETTLERS WALKED TO NORTH AMERICA FROM ASIA. During the last ice age, the ocean was lower, and a wide strip of land connected what are now Alaska and Russia. Thousands of years ago, these early people may have walked across this land bridge carrying stone-tipped spears and wearing warm fur robes.

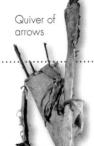

Quiver of arrows

c. 500 CE ▶

People in North Dakota begin using bows and arrows

c. 800

People in North Dakota begin planting corn

c. 1600

Dakota groups begin moving west

FIRST PEOPLE FIRST PEOPLE FIRST PE

Mammoths during the last ice age

A spear point made from Knife River flint

HUMANS ARRIVE

Over thousands of years, people made their way southward and eastward. As the last great ice sheet over North America began to recede about 15,000 years ago, these early settlers followed the edge of the glaciers into what is now North Dakota. Great forests grew in the cool, damp climate near the glaciers. As the ice receded, the climate grew warmer and drier. What is now North Dakota became a land with lakes, rivers, grasslands, and plenty of big animals for early people to hunt, including mammoths, mastodons, and a large species of bison.

Ancient people found a kind of stone, called Knife River flint, in what is now North Dakota. They used the dark tan flint, which breaks like glass, to make sharp tools.

CHANGING LIFEWAYS

Archaeologists study the sites of prehistoric villages and campgrounds to learn about the people who once lived in North Dakota. They have found postholes for houses, stone spear points and arrowheads, pieces of pottery, stone and bone tools, and the ashes of ancient cooking fires. By studying this evidence, archaeologists have learned that about 8,000 years ago, mammoths and other big animals became extinct in the North Dakota area. People soon began relying more on small game, such as deer, rabbits, and a smaller species of bison. They also ate more plants.

PLAINS WOODLAND CULTURE

Beginning around 500 BCE, people in the forested areas of what are now North Dakota and Minnesota learned skills that made their lives much easier. Archaeologists call the time from about 500 BCE to 1000 CE the Woodland period. During this time, Native Americans learned to plant seeds to grow gourds, sunflowers, and other crops. They lived in small villages. In fall and winter, they hunted bison, deer, and elk.

Between 100 BCE and 300 CE, they began to trade with other Native groups to the south and east. They traded Knife River flint and corn for items such as weapons and decorations made of copper and sea-shells. As they traded goods, different groups also exchanged ideas. People along the Red River of the North were influenced by the Adena culture, which was centered in Ohio. The Adena people built large mounds made of earth, which they used for ceremonies and as burial sites. People living in today's North Dakota along the Missouri River were influenced by the Mississippian culture, a complex society in the

Archaeologists have found Knife River flint tools as far east as New York State and as far south as New Mexico. This indicates that Knife River flint was an important trade item among ancient people.

WORD TO KNOW

archaeologists *people who study the remains of past human societies*

Woodland bowl

Mound Builders gathering their crops of corn and squash

Mississippi River valley that also built earth mounds for burials. As evidence of the influence of these groups, archaeologists have found burial mounds near Devils Lake and elsewhere in North Dakota.

Around 500 CE, people in North Dakota learned to hunt with bows and arrows, which was more effective than hunting with spears. They began planting corn around 800.

Native people in what is now North Dakota developed two different lifestyles. Along the banks of the Red and Missouri rivers, people farmed and lived in permanent villages. On the Great Plains in western North Dakota, the people were nomadic, moving from place to place in search of bison.

NATIVE AMERICAN FARMERS

At least 1,000 years ago, people built cities and villages along the Missouri and other rivers. Some of these cities were home to as many as 2,000 people. The people lived in round earth lodges. The walls and roofs were made of poles covered with **sod** to keep out the wind and cold of winter. These Native American farmers planted crops in the fertile soil using hoes made of bison shoulder blades and rakes from deer and elk antlers. With pointed sticks, they planted squash and beans between rows of corn. They also planted some tobacco, which was used in ceremonies.

Picture Yourself...

in a Mandan Earth Lodge

You live along the banks of the Missouri River in a snug earth lodge with a fire pit in the center. On a chilly night, you sit with your brothers and sisters beside the fire pit on a mat of woven plants. The aromas from bison meat, corn, and beans cooking in clay pots make your mouth water. Your mother comes in and hangs deerskin clothing over the fire pit to dry in the smoky heat. Your parents teach you to help keep the earth lodge neat by storing your things in rawhide containers on wooden platforms. At night, you sleep in a bed made of soft prairie grass covered with hides. Your deerskin pillow is stuffed with sweet-smelling herbs.

WORD TO KNOW

sod *soil thickly packed together with grass and roots*

Inside an earth lodge, a Mandan chief tells legends of his people.

SEE IT HERE!

KNIFE RIVER INDIAN VILLAGES NATIONAL HISTORIC SITE

This 1,759-acre (712-hectare) park just north of Stanton preserves sites of Native American villages that date back at least 1,000 years. These villages served as a trading center for Knife River flint. Native American farming also developed in the area. The park contains a replica of an earth lodge, where visitors can see objects that Native people used in daily life.

Women and girls were responsible for growing crops. They sang to the plants to help them grow. They sat on platforms in the fields making noises to scare away animals that would try to eat the crops. Men and boys fished and hunted.

North Dakota's early farmers stored food for winter. They kept corn and beans in underground pits inside their lodges and made flour by grinding corn between two big stones. Archaeologists believe these farmers were the ancestors of three modern Native American nations: the Mandan, Hidatsa, and Arikara peoples.

BISON HUNTERS

The people who lived on the Great Plains of western North Dakota and beyond had a different lifestyle. They

A Hidatsa village on the Knife River

Native American Peoples

(Before European Contact)

This map shows the general area of Native American peoples before
European settlers arrived.

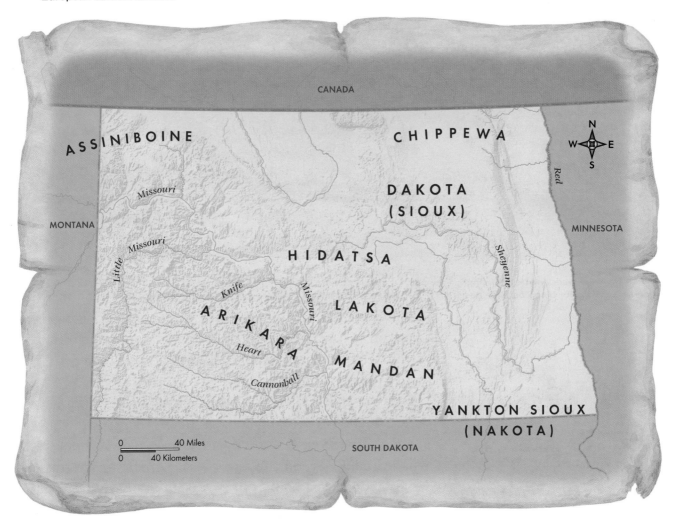

did not have permanent homes. Instead, they moved
from place to place, following great herds of bison.
In addition to hunting bison for food, plains dwellers
gathered nuts, seeds, and other parts of plants. They
lived in tipis, cone-shaped tents made of bison hides.

When Native Americans began using horses, hunting for bison became easier.

Archaeologists have found circles of stones in many places on the Great Plains. They think the stones held down the skin covering of tipis, so they call the circles tipi rings.

When they moved, they packed up all their belongings, including their tipis. They pulled some of their belongings on a travois, a kind of sled made of bison skin stretched between two poles. Everyone, even the dogs, had to carry something.

It was hard to hunt bison on foot, so the hunters often did not have enough to eat. In the 1500s, however, Spaniards arrived in Mexico with horses. Slowly, horses made their way northward. Native American groups in the Southwest bought horses from the Spaniards or found horses that had escaped. They traded some of the horses to groups farther north. By the mid-1700s, horses had spread as far north as North Dakota and had become an important part of life on the plains. Riding swift ponies, Native Americans were able to chase and kill enough bison that they had plenty of food and warm bison robes to trade for other goods.

THE DAKOTA NATION

Around 1600, another group, called the Dakota people, moved into forested areas of what are now Minnesota and eastern North Dakota. The Dakota Nation probably came from woodlands to the east. They paddled birchbark canoes along streams and rivers, fished, and gathered wild rice. They lived a peaceful life until the Ojibwa, or Chippewa, came from the east and forced them to move.

As Europeans began to settle around the Great Lakes in the late 1600s and early 1700s, the Ojibwa people moved westward. They had provided Europeans with valuable beaver pelts in exchange for guns, and these weapons helped Ojibwas push Dakotas and other peoples out of Minnesota and the Red River Valley and onto the plains. Europeans called the Dakota people Sioux, a French word that came from the Ojibwa name for the Dakota, meaning "snake."

As they were pushed westward, Dakota Sioux had to adjust to life on the plains. They split into three main groups: Dakotas, Nakotas, and Lakotas. The Dakota people moved onto the prairies of southwestern Minnesota. Nakotas, sometimes known as Yanktons or Yanktonais, settled on the Drift Prairie, where they farmed part of the year and hunted part of the year. Lakotas settled on the Great Plains, where they learned to ride horses and became great fighters and bison hunters. Over time, the Lakota group became the largest Sioux nation. But soon, life would change even for the powerful Lakota, as European Americans began to spread out over their land.

Picture Yourself . . .

Playing Lakota Games

Life is not easy for you and your family on the Great Plains. Everyone, including you and your brothers and sisters, must do their part. When you finish your work, however, you have time for fun. Your sister plays with a ringtoss toy. She picks up a pointed stick with a cord tied to it and a ring attached to the end of the cord. With a look of intense concentration, she steadies herself and then swings the cord so that the ring flies into the air and lands around the end of the stick. Perfect! Meanwhile, your brother heads out to play snow snakes with his friends. They cut grooves in the snow and send their snakes—long polished sticks—shooting along the grooves to see which travels the farthest.

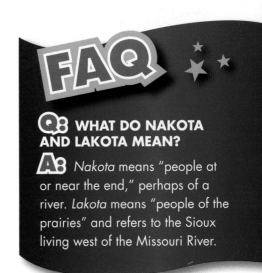

FAQ

Q8 WHAT DO NAKOTA AND LAKOTA MEAN?

A8 *Nakota* means "people at or near the end," perhaps of a river. *Lakota* means "people of the prairies" and refers to the Sioux living west of the Missouri River.

The Rocky Mountains proved to be a challenge for European explorers.

1738

The first Europeans reach today's North Dakota

1780s ▲

The fur trade begins along the Upper Missouri River

1804

Lewis and Clark spend the winter at Fort Mandan

CHAPTER THREE

EXPLORATION AND SETTLEMENT

★

I N THE 1730s AND 1740s, THE FIRST EUROPEAN EXPLORERS ARRIVED IN WHAT IS NOW NORTH DAKOTA FROM CANADA. Like many other European explorers, they were searching for a river that would lead to the Pacific Ocean. They wanted to find a water route to Asia, where Europeans were competing for the lucrative trade in silks and spices. Instead, the first Europeans to reach North Dakota found a vast prairie that ended at a towering mountain range, the Rockies.

1818

The first school in North Dakota opens at Pembina

c. 1850 ▶

Métis invent Red River carts to carry goods on the Pembina Trail to Minnesota

1861

The United States creates the Dakota Territory

European Exploration of North Dakota

The colored arrows on this map show the routes taken by explorers between 1738 and 1805.

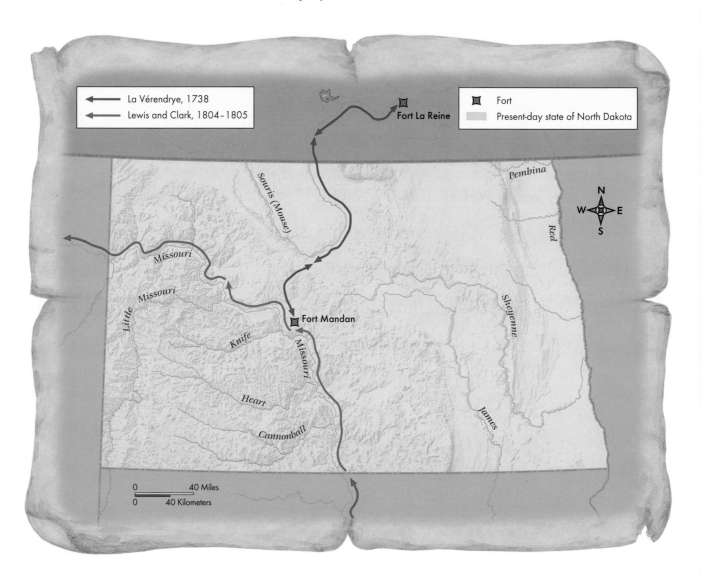

La Vérendrye, 1738
Lewis and Clark, 1804–1805

Fort La Reine

Fort

Present-day state of North Dakota

Souris (Mouse)

Pembina

Red

Missouri

Little Missouri

Knife

Fort Mandan

Missouri

Sheyenne

Heart

Cannonball

James

0   40 Miles
0   40 Kilometers

EUROPEANS ARRIVE

A French Canadian explorer, Pierre Gaultier de La Vérendrye, led the first group of Europeans to see what is now North Dakota. In 1738, his party of about 50 men traveled west from a trading post near what is now Winnipeg, Manitoba, until they came to a Mandan village along the Missouri River.

Although this was the first time that Europeans had seen Mandans in the region, Mandans and other Native Americans in the area had long known about the Europeans. They had acquired axes, metal pots, guns, ammunition, and other European goods from the Assiniboine people, a group that broke away from the Dakota Nation. Assiniboines bought these goods from British traders and, in turn, traded them to Mandans. The Mandan people paid for the goods with corn, tobacco, and bison robes painted with beautiful designs.

La Vérendrye left the Mandan village after 10 days and never returned to North Dakota. In 1742 and 1743, his sons continued along the Upper Missouri and discovered not the Pacific Ocean but the Rocky Mountains. For almost 50 years after that, Europeans showed little interest in this land so remote from their settlements.

PIERRE GAULTIER DE LA VÉRENDRYE: EXPLORER OF THE PLAINS

Pierre Gaultier de La Vérendrye (1685–1749), who was born in Canada, was one of the first explorers to see the northern Great Plains. Even as a boy, he sought adventure, joining the French army when he was only 14 years old. After fighting battles in Europe and North America, he worked as a farmer and fur trader. He convinced the French government that he could find a route to the Pacific Ocean through Lake Winnipeg and a great river beyond. While searching, he set up eight fur-trading posts and went as far west as the Upper Missouri River in North Dakota.

 **Want to know more?** See www.collectionscanada.gc.ca/explorers/h24-1530-e.html

Native Americans trapped animals and traded the furs with Europeans.

COMPETING FOR THE FUR TRADE

It was beaver that brought Europeans to North Dakota because its fur was in high demand in Europe. In the 1700s, tall beaver hats were all the rage for well-dressed men. As a result, the British, French, and Spanish began to compete for North Dakota's fur trade. At various times, all three countries claimed at least part of the land that became North Dakota. Because North Dakota was so far from the colonial capitals, fur traders paid little attention to who claimed the land.

The British began trading for fur with Hidatsas and Mandans on the Upper Missouri River in the 1780s. The French did the same in the 1790s. Spain tried to put a stop to this trade by sending its own traders from St. Louis up the Missouri River. Their effort failed because the distance was so great.

THE LEWIS AND CLARK EXPEDITION

In 1775, colonies on the east coast of North America rebelled against being ruled by Great Britain. By 1783, these colonies had won their independence, and the United States was born. A new nation was now competing for control of North America.

In 1803, U.S. president Thomas Jefferson bought the Louisiana region from France. This vast territory stretched from the Mississippi River to the Rocky Mountains. Jefferson wanted to establish U.S. ownership over the region, wrest control of the fur trade from the British, and find a water route to the Pacific Ocean. He asked Congress to fund an **expedition** to the West.

WORD TO KNOW

expedition *a trip for the purpose of exploration*

Native American guide Sacagawea with explorers Meriwether Lewis and William Clark

Louisiana Purchase

This map shows the area (in yellow) that made up the Louisiana Purchase and the present-day state of North Dakota (in orange).

British Possessions

Louisiana Purchase

Spanish Possessions

N
W · E
S

United States, 1803

Louisiana Purchase

United States Territory, 1803

Present-day state of North Dakota

WORD TO KNOW

corps *a group working together on a special mission*

After Congress approved his plan, he chose two U.S. Army officers, Meriwether Lewis and William Clark, to lead the expedition.

In May 1804, Lewis and Clark's **Corps** of Discovery set out from St. Louis. The party headed up the Missouri River in a large, flat-bottomed boat and two canoes. They brought along supplies, scientific instruments, and gifts for the Native Americans. In October, they reached the Mandan and Hidatsa villages near what is now Bismarck. There they built a fort where they could spend the winter. That winter, they met a Native American woman named Sacagawea, who joined the Corps of Discovery. She became important to the expedition, working as a translator with Native Americans.

Assisting Sacagawea was an enslaved African man named York, whom Clark had owned since childhood. York learned new languages easily. He was also an excellent hunter and fisher, and he was skilled at frontier survival. Like Sacagawea, he served as an ambassador of goodwill to the many Native American nations the corps encountered.

It took more than two years for Lewis and Clark to cross the continent to the Pacific Ocean and then return to St. Louis. Along the way, they encouraged peaceful relations with Native American groups. They

SACAGAWEA: TRANSLATOR FOR LEWIS AND CLARK

Sacagawea (1786?–1812) was a member of the Shoshone Nation, but as a child, she was kidnapped from her home in Idaho by Hidatsas and brought to their village on the Missouri River. There a French trader, Toussaint Charbonneau, gained ownership of her. Lewis and Clark hired the couple as interpreters. When the group arrived in Shoshone territory, Sacagawea met Native Americans led by her brother. She and her brother helped the explorers buy horses and find a guide through the Rockies. She also gathered plants for food and medicine, proving herself a vital member of the expedition. Today her statue (shown here) stands in front of the North Dakota Heritage Center.

? **Want to know more?** See www.usmint.gov/mint_programs/golden_dollar_coin/index.cfm?action=sacAbout

This compass was used on the Lewis and Clark expedition.

told Native people that the U.S. government would send traders with all the supplies they needed as long as they kept the peace. The explorers also convinced the Indians to trade with Americans rather than the British.

WOW

Lewis and Clark spent more time in North Dakota than in any other place they visited on their expedition.

SEE IT HERE!

FORT MANDAN

In the fall of 1804, the Lewis and Clark expedition built a fort at today's Washburn where they spent the winter. This fort has now been re-created to bring to life the experience of exploring the American West. The captain's quarters hold Lewis's field desk and Clark's instruments for making maps. In the enlisted men's rooms, it is easy to imagine members of the corps huddled around stone fireplaces and wrapped in bison robes as the temperatures plunged to –45°F (–43°C).

In 1837, a number of Mandans died from smallpox, a disease brought to the region by Europeans.

EXPANDING THE FUR TRADE

The fur trade on the Missouri grew rapidly after the Lewis and Clark expedition. In the 1830s, fur traders built posts such as Fort Clark near Hidatsa and Mandan villages. Steamboats carried goods for trading up the Missouri and brought furs back.

European fur traders also brought something else to the Native Americans—smallpox. Several times, smallpox epidemics struck the plains Indians. Infected passengers on a steamboat in 1837 brought the disease to Fort Clark, and Mandans living there were almost wiped out.

By this time, North Dakota's first permanent European settlement, Pembina, had been established in the Red River Valley. In 1803, two rival fur-trading companies had established posts at what became Pembina. A number of Métis, people descended from both Europeans and Native Americans, also lived there. In 1812, some Scottish settlers arrived at Pembina. That same year, the United States and Great Britain again went to war in the War of 1812. Six years later, the two nations made boundary agreements through the Convention of 1818. This set the official border between the United States and Canada. Pembina and other parts of the Red River Valley fell within the United States, and the Scottish settlers moved north to what is now Winnipeg, Canada. The Métis, however, stayed on and opened a new fur-trading route called the Pembina Trail.

Travel over the prairie was difficult until the Métis invented the Red River cart. These simple carts had gigantic wheels and were usually pulled by oxen. The wheels had broad rims that did not easily sink into the soft prairie soil. Because the carts were made entirely of wood, they were easily repaired. But their axles were never greased, so they made a tremendous racket.

By 1850, trains of Red River carts, their wheels screeching, hauled bison robes and a type of dried food called pemmican over the Pembina Trail to St. Paul, Minnesota. The Red River carts and the trails they traveled, along with steamboats that came up the Missouri and Red rivers, provided links between North Dakota and the rest of the United States.

DAKOTA TERRITORY

Congress created the Dakota Territory in 1861. At first, the territory contained land that would make up parts

WOW

Roman Catholic missionaries in Pembina opened the first school in North Dakota in 1818.

FAQ

Q: WHAT IS PEMMICAN?

A: Native Americans made this concentrated food from dried bison, elk, or deer meat mixed with fat and dried cranberries.

A U.S. government exploring party sets up its tent near a Native American camp on the Red River of the North, 1854.

of the future states of Montana and Wyoming. Montana became a separate territory in 1864, and Wyoming did so in 1868. At that point, the Dakota Territory was made up only of today's North Dakota and South Dakota.

In the 1850s, Native Americans had signed treaties with the U.S. government, giving up large areas of land in Minnesota in exchange for smaller reservation lands and payments of supplies and money. Often, however, government agents and private traders failed to deliver payments of either supplies or money. Dakotas in Minnesota, starving and feeling betrayed by broken government promises, rose up against white settlers. Some Dakotas who were not captured fled into Dakota Territory, and the U.S. military chased after them. Riding in columns on horseback, U.S. Army troops appeared on the plains. Dakotas and army soldiers fought major battles in 1863 and 1864. The army then began building a chain of forts to protect white settlers heading west and workers who had arrived to build railroads.

Meanwhile, hunters killed off bison at an astonishing speed. Between 1870 and 1880, white hunters killed some 30 million bison on the Great Plains.

The Lakota people saw what had happened to the Dakota Nation and that white hunters were killing the bison, which they depended on for food, clothing, and shelter. They became increasingly concerned that white Americans threatened their way of life. In one treaty after another, the U.S. government promised lands to Native Americans, but then white settlers trespassed on their land, breaking the treaties. As events would soon prove, the Lakota people were right to be concerned.

Fort Rice, one of the many forts built to protect settlers in Dakota Territory

READ ABOUT

Workers building the Northern Pacific Railway, 1880s

1873

The first railroad across North Dakota reaches the Missouri River

1874

Prospectors invade Lakota land after gold is discovered in the Black Hills

1874–1876 ▲

Sitting Bull and other Lakotas resist being forced onto reservations

CHAPTER FOUR

GROWTH AND CHANGE

★

USING SLEDGEHAMMERS AND SHOVELS, WORKERS LAID RAILROAD TRACKS ACROSS NORTH DAKOTA. In 1870, work on the Northern Pacific Railway began in Minnesota, and the tracks reached the Missouri River by 1873. Towns sprang up along the route, filled with post offices, stores, and other services.

1880s

Theodore Roosevelt establishes ranches in the Badlands

1886–1887

Blizzards destroy cattle herds in the Badlands

1889 ▶

North Dakota becomes the 39th state

Soldiers, with wagons and weapons, cross the plains of Dakota Territory during the Black Hills expedition of 1874.

The first public school in North Dakota opened in Bismarck in 1873.

WORDS TO KNOW

cavalry *soldiers who fight on horseback*

prospectors *people who explore a region searching for valuable minerals*

BATTLING FOR THEIR LAND

The first railroad town in North Dakota was Fargo, where a railroad bridge crossed the Red River, which separates Minnesota from North Dakota. By treaty, the lands west of the Red River belonged to the Lakota Nation and other Native American groups. Native Americans, who saw railroad workers as trespassing on their land, sometimes attacked the workers. The workers asked that more soldiers be sent to the forts along the Missouri River to protect them. One of the most important outposts was Fort Rice, where a young officer named George Armstrong Custer commanded the Seventh U.S. **Cavalry**.

In 1874, Custer led an expedition to explore the Black Hills of southern Dakota Territory. He reported finding gold in the streams there, and his report set off a gold rush. **Prospectors** poured into the Black Hills.

But the Black Hills were sacred to the Lakota people, and by treaty the United States had granted the hills to the Lakota. At first, the U.S. government tried to stop the miners from entering the Black Hills. Then the government tried to buy the land, but the Lakota Nation refused to sell. Finally, the government disregarded the treaty and ordered all Lakotas onto reservations. U.S. troops rounded up those Lakotas who refused to go or who did not hear the order.

Two Lakota leaders, Sitting Bull and Crazy Horse, led the resistance to this effort to take over Indian lands. More than 3,000 of their followers camped together in Montana Territory. Custer and the cavalry, then stationed at Fort Abraham Lincoln in northern Dakota Territory, joined other army units trying to defeat the Lakota forces. In an 1876 battle on the Little Bighorn River in Montana, remembered as Custer's Last Stand, Crazy Horse and his men killed Custer and his entire command.

Crazy Horse

In response, thousands of soldiers went to the Great Plains to round up all the Native Americans. The army forces included units of African American soldiers whom the Native Americans called Buffalo Soldiers. Slowly, Native Americans were moved off their land.

THE GREAT DAKOTA LAND BOOM

The government had given the Northern Pacific Railway huge amounts of land along the tracks. The railroad planned to sell the land to pay for laying the rails. To find settlers, the Northern Pacific sent recruiters to Europe. Soon people began coming into the Dakota Territory from Norway, Germany, and Sweden as well as the United States and Canada.

The Northern Pacific ran out of money in 1873, when the railroad reached the Missouri River. The cost

In an effort to attract more German immigrants, the Northern Pacific Railway named a town along the Missouri River Bismarck, in honor of German chancellor Otto von Bismarck.

48

Bonanza farms needed a lot of workers to plant and harvest crops.

FAQ ★ ★ ★

Q8 WHAT WAS THE BIGGEST BONANZA FARM?

A8 The Grandin Brothers Farm was made of about 75,000 acres (30,351 ha) of land. It also had a fleet of steamboats for shipping grain to the flour mills.

of laying the tracks was more than anyone had anticipated. The company could not pay back its big investors with money, so railroad officials came up with a plan to pay the investors with huge tracts of land. The investors set up big farms, which became known as bonanza farms.

Two railroad officials started the first bonanza farm on 13,000 acres (5,261 ha) in the Red River Valley. The farm employed 400 workers. The land and climate were ideal for growing spring wheat, a type of wheat well-suited for making bread. Soon the idea spread around the world that it was possible to make a fortune growing wheat on bonanza farms. Investors bought land and workers flocked to the Dakota Territory. Between

1879 and 1886, the population of what would soon be North Dakota increased by about 100,000 people. Many of them set up small homesteads, but many others worked on the bonanza farms.

Some 90 bonanza farms eventually operated in the Red River Valley and the Drift Prairie to the west. The investors hired experienced managers to oversee the farms. The managers hired thousands of seasonal workers to do the plowing, planting, and harvesting in the warm months. The workers lived in bunkhouses and had to obey strict rules. They worked 13 hours a day driving mules and breaking up the sod. The bonanza farms also employed women to cook and do laundry for the field hands. But once the wheat was harvested, the farm managers did not need the workers until the planting season the following year. The wheat was simply loaded onto railroad cars and carried to mills in Minneapolis, where it was ground.

AFRICAN AMERICANS IN NORTH DAKOTA

Slavery was never permitted in Dakota Territory, and North Dakota did not become a state until slavery was banned throughout the nation. Nevertheless, some early explorers and traders brought enslaved people with them, and some African Americans worked as fur traders in the early days of North Dakota.

Later, African American Buffalo Soldiers performed many duties in North Dakota, including helping guard Northern Pacific trains. Some African Americans also traveled to the Black Hills to prospect for gold. In 1870, Dakota Territory was home to 94 African Americans. Many were farmers, while others owned restaurants, ran their own churches, or worked as barbers or cooks.

SEE IT HERE!

BONANZAVILLE

The Cass County Historical Society has gathered buildings from all over North Dakota to show how people lived during earlier eras, including the time of the bonanza farms. This outdoor museum in West Fargo includes a bonanza farmhouse and the first log house in Fargo. Visitors can see a wagon that served as a kitchen for wheat-threshing crews, as well as a blacksmith shop, a drugstore, a courthouse, and a town hall. Bonanzaville also features a museum that displays Native American tools and clothing.

Buffalo Soldier

Members of an African American community in Williston, 1920

An African American named Sarah Campbell worked as a servant with Custer's party when they explored the Black Hills in 1874. She stayed on to cook for miners and claimed to be the first non-Native woman in the Black Hills. Another African American, Isaiah Dorman, died with Custer at the Battle of the Little Bighorn. Dorman was married to a Lakota woman and was friendly toward Native Americans. Custer brought him along as an interpreter and scout.

In the early 1900s, the Thompson family established a farm near Driscoll, just east of Bismarck. Their daughter Era Bell became a writer and editor. She wrote a book called *American Daughter*, which discussed growing up in North Dakota, a place where few white people had ever seen an African American. She told how out of place she felt and about the racial **prejudice** she faced. One Christmas, her family traveled 30 miles (48 km) to be with two other African American families. When they sat down to eat, "there were fifteen of us," she said, "four percent of the state's entire [black] population."

BADLANDS RANCHING

While the bonanza farms thrived along the Red River, cattle ranchers discovered the grazing land along the Little Missouri River in the Badlands. Soon there were big ranches with thousands of cattle. The ranchers did not own the land where the cattle grazed. Instead, they shared it, and once a year there was a roundup to sort out the cattle. One of the ranchers in the Badlands was Theodore Roosevelt, who would one day be president of the United States.

As ranchers brought in more and more cattle, Roosevelt worried that the land was being overgrazed. Then came the frigid winter of 1886–1887, when a November blizzard was followed by subzero cold.

MINI-BIO

ERA BELL THOMPSON: AMERICAN DAUGHTER

Era Bell Thompson (1905–1986) was born in Iowa and moved to Driscoll with her family in 1914. As a young North Dakota farm girl, she busted broncos with her brothers and made friends with the German and Norwegian families living nearby. While studying at the University of North Dakota, she set five state women's track records. Her special talent, however, was with words, and in 1933 she moved to Chicago and began her career as a journalist. Her book, *American Daughter*, helped her land a job with *Ebony* magazine. She worked there the rest of her life as co-managing editor and then international editor.

? Want to know more? See www.mandanhistory.org/biographieslz/erabellthompson.html

WORD TO KNOW

prejudice *an unreasonable hatred or fear of others based on race, religion, ethnic group, gender, or other factors*

WORKING THE ROUNDUP

Theodore Roosevelt established two ranches in the Badlands in the 1880s, and he thoroughly enjoyed the work. He wrote his sister, "I have been on the roundup for [two weeks] and really enjoy the work greatly; in fact I am passing a most pleasant summer. . . . We breakfast at three every morning, and work from sixteen to eighteen hours a day, counting night guard; so I get pretty sleepy; but I feel strong as a bear."

Severe weather continued throughout the winter, and by spring three-quarters of all the cattle in the Badlands had died. Roosevelt and many others gave up the life of a cowboy.

WOUNDED KNEE

By the late 1880s, most Lakotas had been crowded onto reservations. The final encounter between the Lakota people and the U.S. Army took place at Wounded Knee Creek in 1890 on the Pine Ridge Reservation in today's South Dakota. A new religion called the Ghost Dance was spreading on the reservations, where Native Americans were starving. The Ghost Dance religion taught that soon

U.S. soldiers fight Lakotas at the Wounded Knee Massacre, 1890.

the bison and antelope would return, that there would be no more hunger or disease, that soldiers' bullets would not hurt Native Americans, and that Native Americans would once again roam freely on the land. In the Ghost Dance ceremony, Lakotas chanted and danced around a circle until they were exhausted, in preparation for the changes that would come.

The U.S. government, fearing a rebellion, outlawed this dancing and sent troops to the reservations to enforce the ban. During this effort, Sitting Bull, who was living on the Standing Rock Reservation along the border of present-day North Dakota and South Dakota, was shot and killed. About 350 of his followers—men, women, and children—fled to Wounded Knee Creek. U.S. troops followed them and opened fire on the Indians, although no one is sure why. They fought back, but when it was over, about 300 Native Americans had been killed in what is called the Wounded Knee Massacre. Ghost Dancing had failed to protect the Lakota people. The massacre marked the end of the fighting between the U.S. government and Native Americans on the northern plains.

MINI-BIO

SITTING BULL: LAKOTA LEADER

Sitting Bull (c. 1831–1890) was a Lakota holy man and leader who was revered for his bravery. He led his troops in several battles against the U.S. Army after the United States had violated treaties it had made with Native Americans. In the fight to drive out gold prospectors who had invaded the Black Hills, he helped defeat George Armstrong Custer at the Battle of the Little Bighorn. But finally, unable to feed his followers, Sitting Bull agreed to move to a reservation in 1881. U.S. officials feared Sitting Bull might join the Ghost Dance movement, so they sent soldiers and Lakota police to arrest him. Sitting Bull's fighters tried to protect him, a gunfight broke out, and Sitting Bull was killed.

? Want to know more? See www.pbs.org/weta/thewest/people/s_z/sittingbull.htm

People from around the world came to North Dakota to build homes and farm the land.

STATEHOOD AND IMMIGRATION

Meanwhile, the residents of Dakota Territory wanted statehood. They asked that the territory be divided into two states, because the centers of population were on opposite ends of the territory. About 190,000 people lived in the northern Dakota Territory, and more than 340,000 lived in the south. On November 2, 1889, President Benjamin Harrison signed a bill creating North Dakota as the 39th state and South Dakota as the 40th state.

After North Dakota became a state, another wave of newcomers arrived. Some came to set up farms. The Homestead Act promised 160 acres (65 ha) of land to any U.S. citizen (who was at least 21 and the head of a family) who would build a house and farm and live there for five years. Other North Dakota settlers bought up land that had once been part of bonanza farms. Many of the new settlers came from Scandinavian countries,

North Dakota: From Territory to Statehood

(1868–1889)

This map shows the Dakota Territory (outlined in green) and the area (in yellow) that became the state of North Dakota in 1889.

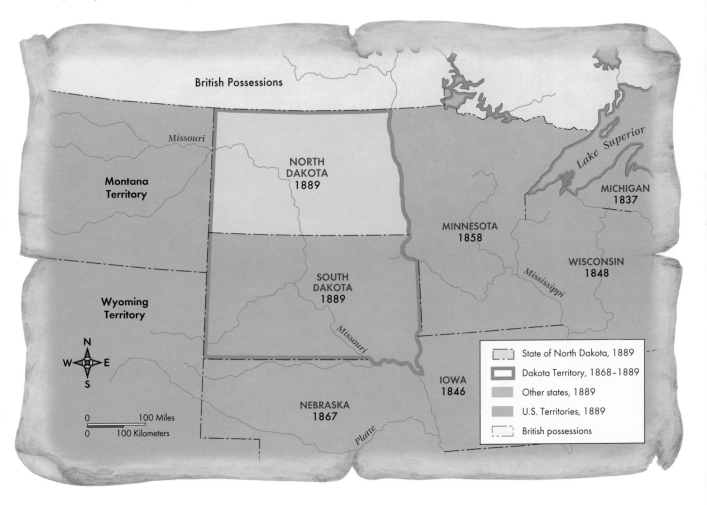

British Possessions

Missouri

Montana Territory

NORTH DAKOTA 1889

MINNESOTA 1858

Lake Superior

MICHIGAN 1837

WISCONSIN 1848

Mississippi

Wyoming Territory

SOUTH DAKOTA 1889

Missouri

N W E S

0   100 Miles
0   100 Kilometers

IOWA 1846

NEBRASKA 1867

Platte

State of North Dakota, 1889	
Dakota Territory, 1868–1889	
Other states, 1889	
U.S. Territories, 1889	
British possessions	

especially Norway. By the early 1900s, approximately 25 percent of North Dakota's population had been born in a foreign country. In the coming years, they would work together to improve life for everyone in their new home.

READ ABOUT

A view of
Broadway in
Fargo, 1920s

1915 ▲
*Arthur C. Townley founds
the Nonpartisan League*

1919
*State-owned
businesses are
established*

1930s
*Severe drought strikes
the Great Plains*

MORE MODERN TIMES

★

A S THE 20TH CENTURY BEGAN, NORTH DAKOTA WANTED TO GROW. But many companies in Minnesota owned the railroads, banks, flour mills, and grain elevators used by North Dakotans. Eventually, taxes were lowered and regulations were adjusted to attract new businesses. As a result, lignite mines, brickworks, and flour mills began operating in the state.

▲ **1941–1945**
Lakota and Dakota code talkers help win World War II

1947
Construction begins on Garrison Dam

2007
Oil companies begin drilling in western North Dakota

Farmers in Walsh County with a thresher and water wagon, early 1900s

FARMERS ORGANIZE

Many ordinary North Dakotans believed that big corporations were given too many advantages at the expense of farmers and workers. Farmers, for example, resented the high rates they had to pay railroads to ship their wheat to grain elevators. When farmers sold the wheat, they suspected that the grain elevator operators cheated them out of money by not weighing the wheat properly. Farmers also protested that their taxes were too high and that they were unable to get fair loans from Minnesota banks. North Dakotans came to bitterly resent big corporations.

When the United States entered World War I in 1917, some North Dakotans were strongly opposed. They claimed that businesses were seeking profits through the war. Nevertheless, almost 32,000 North Dakotans served in the military forces and more than 1,300 lost their lives.

A spirit of political independence and rebellion was growing in North Dakota. In 1915, farm families in the state had formed a new organization called the Nonpartisan League. By 1918, the Nonpartisan League was the most powerful organization in North Dakota, with some 40,000 members. The league called for many reforms, including a state-owned bank, mill, and grain elevator. It also favored giving women the right to vote.

The league used the main political parties to reach its goals. Most North Dakotans in the early 1900s voted for Republican Party candidates. The league ran its own Republican candidates and by 1919 had taken control of the state government. The state legislature in 1919 passed all the league proposals, including the establishment of state-owned businesses and an industrial commission to oversee them. Governor Lynn J. Frazier, a league member, signed the bills into law.

Soon, however, members of the league began to fight among themselves. Some farmers, suffering from low crop prices, could not pay back their mortgage loans. The state-owned Bank of North Dakota **foreclosed** on some farms. When the bank took their farms, the farmers felt betrayed. Opponents of the league formed an organization called the Independent Voters Association (IVA), which accused league leaders of not being

MINI-BIO

ARTHUR C. TOWNLEY: NONPARTISAN LEAGUE FOUNDER

Arthur C. Townley (1880–1959), the founder of the Nonpartisan League, was a successful farmer in North Dakota. After bad weather and falling grain prices wiped out his farm, he began working for the Socialist Party. He drove to remote farming regions to talk with farmers about his belief that the railroads and corporations were cheating them. He urged farmers to join the Nonpartisan League. In 1922, he was arrested for working against the World War I (1914–1918) effort. In the years to come, Townley lost popularity and supported himself as a salesman.

? Want to know more? See www.prairiepublic.org/programs/datebook/bydate/06/1206/121506.jsp

WORDS TO KNOW

Socialist Party *a political group that favors socialism, a political system based on shared or governmental ownership of the production and distribution of goods*

foreclosed *took back property because payment was overdue*

Members of a North Dakota family during the drought of the 1930s

WORD TO KNOW

recall *a vote to remove elected officials from office*

patriotic because they had opposed sending U.S. troops to fight in World War I. The IVA managed to get many of its candidates elected to the legislature and in 1921 forced a **recall** of Frazier and other officials who were supported by the Nonpartisan League. In the 1930s, however, the Nonpartisan League again took control of state government. After the 1930s, the league lost influence with the Republican Party, and in 1956 it joined forces with the state Democratic Party to create the Democratic-NPL Party. Today, the political beliefs of the group are much different.

GOOD TIMES AND TROUBLES

Following World War I, new technology began to change life for North Dakotans. Radio stations began broadcasting in 1922. Radios brought news and entertainment into remote farm homes. North Dakotans could drive to town in automobiles to watch movies in theaters. Gasoline-powered tractors began to replace horse-drawn equipment on country roads.

Wheat farmers faced difficult times in the 1920s as farm prices fell. To help themselves, they formed cooperatives, which are organizations owned jointly by their members who share in the benefits and profits. Some cooperatives were formed to reduce costs. For example, when a cooperative bought large amounts of gasoline and oil at one time, the price was lower. Other cooperatives worked to get higher prices for the crops the farmers grew. The largest cooperative organization was the North Dakota Farmers Union, which formed in 1927.

Farmers were already struggling in the 1920s when in 1929, the prices of **stocks** on the New York Stock Exchange plunged, and the country fell further into the Great Depression. Many wealthy people lost their fortunes, companies shut down, and millions of workers lost their jobs. Many jobless people became homeless because they could not afford to pay rent or pay the loans on their houses.

To make matters worse, during the 1930s a severe drought struck North Dakota and other parts of the Great Plains. Windstorms roared across the plains, scooping up the dry soil and carrying it along as great clouds of black dust. A woman living on the North Dakota plains recorded the terrible times in her diary: "April 25, 1934, Wednesday. . . . Many days this spring the air is just full of dirt coming, literally, for hundreds of miles. It sifts into everything. After we wash the dishes and put them away, so much dirt sifts into the cupboards we must wash them again before the next meal. Clothes in the closets are covered with dust. Last weekend no one was taking an automobile out for fear of ruining the motor."

WORD TO KNOW

stocks *shares in the ownership of a company*

MINI-BIO

WILLIAM "WILD BILL" LANGER: CHAMPION OF FARMERS

William Langer (1886–1959), who was born in Casselton, was a member of the Nonpartisan League and became governor in 1933. He was soon accused of forcing state employees to contribute to his campaign and ordered to leave office. Langer refused, put the state under military law, and hid in the governor's mansion. Eventually, he was forced to leave. After he was found not guilty of the charges against him, he served as governor from 1937 to 1939. He tried to help farmers during the Great Depression through actions such as ordering the state to pay farmers higher prices for wheat. He served in the U.S. Senate from 1941 until his death in 1959.

 Want to know more? See www.nd.gov/hist/ndgov5.htm

To help North Dakotans suffering during the Great Depression, Governor William Langer ordered banks to stop foreclosing on farms. In an effort to raise the price of wheat, he stopped wheat shipments from leaving North Dakota. Despite these efforts, farmers found little relief until the federal government stepped in.

In 1933, President Franklin D. Roosevelt began a series of programs called the New Deal to aid people hurt by the Great Depression. Perhaps 70 percent of North Dakotans needed government help. Federal programs put North Dakotans to work building highways and parks and improving city water supplies. Despite these efforts, thousands of North Dakota families lost their farms, and large corporations bought up their land. Some farmers moved to cities and towns in North Dakota. Others moved out of the state. In 1930, North Dakota's population was 680,845. By 1940, the state's population had dropped to 641,935.

WORLD WAR II

As the 1930s ended, so did the drought. The Depression did not end for North Dakotans, however, until the United States entered World War II. This war began in Europe in 1939, when Germany invaded Poland.

Workers in the Civilian Conservation Corps, a New Deal program, building a bridge at the International Peace Garden, 1936

Great Britain, France, and other nations declared war on Germany, and soon war raged across the continent. Roosevelt wanted to help fight the Germans, but some Americans, including North Dakota senator Gerald P. Nye and Governor William Langer, were opposed to it. They were **isolationists**, who did not want the United States involved with other nations' wars. On December 7, 1941, Japanese planes bombed the U.S. naval fleet in Pearl Harbor, Hawai'i. The United States immediately declared war on Japan and its ally, Germany.

North Dakotans stepped up to do their part in the war. The United States needed to feed hundreds of thousands of troops. North Dakota farmers provided the wheat for making bread, and the price of wheat

WORD TO KNOW

isolationists *people who believe that their country should not become involved with the problems of foreign nations*

MINI-BIO

WOODY KEEBLE: WAR HERO

Woodrow Wilson "Woody" Keeble (1917–1982) was born on the Sisseton-Wahpeton Sioux Reservation in South Dakota but spent most of his life in Wahpeton, North Dakota. During World War II, Keeble and other U.S. troops landed on the Japanese-held island of Guadalcanal. He threw himself into one of the most brutal jungle battles of the war and received medals for his bravery. During the Korean War, he again served his country. He was repeatedly wounded and each time returned to action. In 2008, more than 25 years after his death, Keeble became the first Sioux to be awarded the Medal of Honor, the highest U.S. military decoration.

❓ **Want to know more?** See www.governor.state.nd.us/awards/rr-gallery/keeble.html

rose once again. About 60,000 men and women from North Dakota served in the armed forces during the war, and more than 1,500 lost their lives.

Some Native Americans who joined the army served as "code talkers" during World War II. They received and passed along radio messages using codes based on their own languages. Code talkers worked in more than a dozen Native American languages, including Dakota, Lakota, Nakota, Navajo,

Native American code talkers during World War II

and Comanche. First, a code talker translated a message into his own Native language. Then he coded the translated message and spoke the coded message over the radio to another code talker, who decoded the message and translated it for his fellow soldiers. Very few non-Native people could speak Native American languages. Even if the enemy managed to crack the code used to send the radio messages, the language was unintelligible to them. The enemy listening in was never able to figure out a code talker message. In 2002, Congress passed the Code Talkers Recognition Act to honor the Native American code talkers, whose work saved the lives of thousands of soldiers.

POSTWAR CHANGES

The automobile brought great changes to North Dakota. After the war, many North Dakotans bought cars, which made people living in distant farming communities less isolated. The state and federal governments built roads and highways that crisscrossed the state, connecting rural areas with cities. Trucks used the roads to haul goods, and soon North Dakota did not have to rely completely on the railroads.

In 1947, construction began on Garrison Dam, a project to provide flood control and electricity along the Upper Missouri River. Not everyone was pleased with the project, however. The construction of the dam created Lake Sakakawea, which flooded much fertile farmland along the Missouri River, including about one-fourth of the Fort Berthold Indian Reservation. This land belonged to the Three Affiliated Tribes, made up of Mandans, Hidatsas, and Arikaras. Hundreds of families were forced to leave their homes and farms in the fertile valley and relocate to land on the dry plains.

SEE IT HERE!

GARRISON DAM

Starting in 1947, 9 million truckloads of dirt would be hauled to the Missouri River to build Garrison Dam, one of the largest earthen dams in the world. The dam, which was completed in 1953, rises 210 feet (64 m) high and stretches 2.5 miles (4 km) across the river. Its five generators produce enough electricity to supply a city of 350,000 people for one year. Today, visitors can tour the dam and learn how it produces power. They can also enjoy boating and fishing on the dam's **reservoir**, Lake Sakakawea.

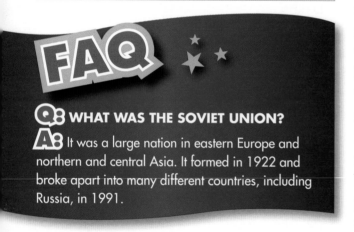

FAQ

Q8 WHAT WAS THE SOVIET UNION?

A8 It was a large nation in eastern Europe and northern and central Asia. It formed in 1922 and broke apart into many different countries, including Russia, in 1991.

WORDS TO KNOW

reservoir *artificial lake or tank for storing water*

strip mines *places where soil or rock is scraped from the earth's surface to reach coal or ores*

synthetic *related to something that doesn't occur in nature*

Just as it had 100 years earlier, the military played a major role in North Dakota in the 1950s and 1960s. At the time, the United States was engaged in a political struggle with the Soviet Union, known as the cold war. During the cold war, the two countries were rivals for military and political power. The U.S. government built the Grand Forks and Minot Air Force bases to house nuclear missiles and long-range bombers that could be used against the Soviet Union.

Energy grew more important to the North Dakota economy in the middle of the 20th century. Oil was discovered near Tioga in 1951, and the mining of lignite expanded in the 1960s. **Strip mines** removed soil to get at the lignite close to the surface, and generating companies built power plants that burned lignite. The mines and power plants, however, raised environmental issues. Many North Dakotans pressed for laws that would require companies to restore land harmed by the mining operations and establish a plan for cutting down on pollution. A new use for lignite appeared in 1984, when a plant opened for converting the coal into cleaner-burning **synthetic** natural gas.

RECENT TIMES

Unpredictable weather and distant events have sometimes given North Dakota a boom-and-bust economy—quick growth that just as quickly disappears. In the

A missile procedure trainer simulates action at a launch control center at the Grand Forks Air Force Base, 1986.

1970s, for example, the U.S. government decided to sell wheat to the Soviet Union, which had previously been banned because of poor relations between the two countries. As a result, North Dakota farmers earned record high prices for grain, and many borrowed money to expand their operations. In the 1980s, world wheat prices dropped, and farmers had trouble repaying their debts. Droughts continued to plague farmers as well.

An oil well operates near a durum wheat field in Tioga, 2008.

A boom-and-bust cycle also hit North Dakota's oil industry. Some geologists estimate that up to 200 billion barrels of oil lie underground in western North Dakota. But the oil is about 2 miles (3 km) down and difficult and expensive to get out. When worldwide oil prices are high, oil companies consider it worthwhile to drill in North Dakota. When oil prices fall, North Dakota oil is considered too expensive.

After oil prices rose in the 1980s, people in Williston believed that oil workers would swell their town's population, so the town borrowed $20 million to pave streets and put in new sewer lines for homes that would need to be built. Then world prices for oil fell and so did the prospect of people moving into Williston. The community was stuck with a huge debt.

Since the 1940s, many North Dakotans with small farms have sold their land to larger farms. The average size of a farm in North Dakota has more than doubled, from about 500 acres (202 ha) to 1,300 acres (526 ha). At the same time, big farm machines do most of the work, so fewer workers are needed for planting and harvesting. With fewer workers, there is less need for retail stores and other services in nearby towns. Businesses have closed, and jobs have disappeared. Between 2000 and 2006, the population of the state decreased by 1 percent, as many young people left North Dakota in search of better opportunities elsewhere.

Many government and business leaders believe that the problem could be addressed by bringing in a greater variety of industries. Leaders have also called for widespread Internet access, better parks, and improved housing. In addition, the state is expanding its tourism industry.

In 2004, world oil prices again began to rise, and oil companies again became interested in North Dakota oil. By 2007, oil workers were crowding into western towns. Some North Dakotans, with a long distrust of big corporations, try not to get too excited about the promise of future riches. They fear another boom-and-bust cycle, but others believe that the state's oil boom will endure and help create new jobs in other industries such as construction and restaurants. Some also hope that technology for using corn to create an alternative fuel called **ethanol** will provide a new source of income for North Dakota farmers and provide the jobs needed to keep young people in the state.

WORD TO KNOW

ethanol *an alcohol used as a gasoline substitute, made by fermenting corn or other material*

70

READ ABOUT

This flutist keeps
the traditions of
his people alive.

CHAPTER SIX

PEOPLE

★

O N THE PLAINS ABOVE THE MISSOURI RIVER, A NATIVE AMERICAN RANCHER RIDES OUT TO CHECK THE TRIBE'S HERD OF BISON. A Norwegian American wheat farmer, whose great-grandfather immigrated to North Dakota to farm the land, climbs up on a giant machine to begin the day's harvest. In Bismarck, a computer programmer heads off to her job in a downtown skyscraper, while in Grand Forks, an African American teacher welcomes a new Hispanic student to class. All of these people call North Dakota home.

Where North Dakotans Live

The colors on this map indicate population density throughout the state. The darker the color, the more people live there.

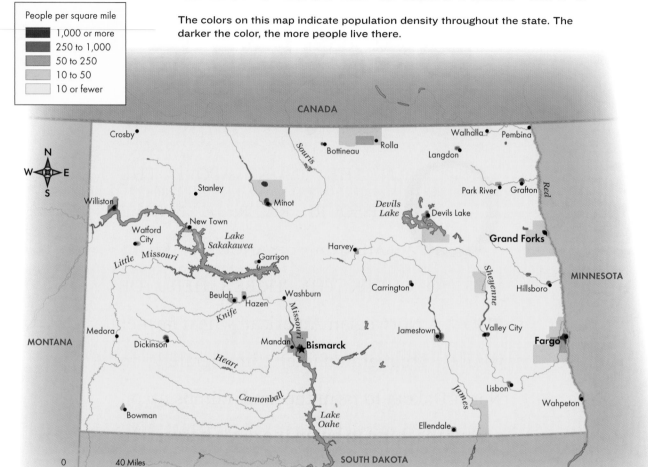

People per square mile

■	1,000 or more
■	250 to 1,000
■	50 to 250
■	10 to 50
■	10 or fewer

Big City Life

This list shows the population of North Dakota's biggest cities.

Fargo 90,672
Bismarck 57,337
Grand Forks 49,792
Minot 34,984
West Fargo 19,487

Source: U.S. Census Bureau, 2006 estimate

ON FARMS AND IN CITIES

If you are looking for plenty of wide-open spaces, then North Dakota is for you. North Dakota is a land of big farms and few people. More people live in Memphis, Tennessee, than in all of North Dakota.

Even though North Dakota is known for its wheat farms and cattle ranches, almost 56 percent of North Dakotans live in cities such as Bismarck, Dickinson,

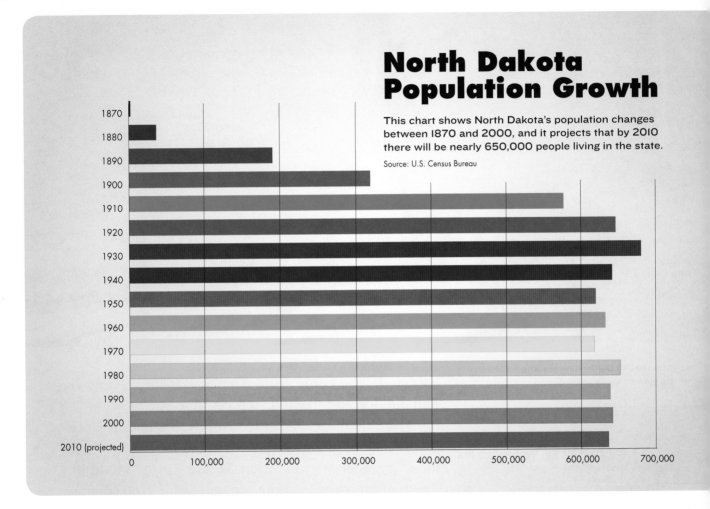

North Dakota Population Growth

This chart shows North Dakota's population changes between 1870 and 2000, and it projects that by 2010 there will be nearly 650,000 people living in the state.

Source: U.S. Census Bureau

Grand Forks, and Fargo. In farm country, there are fewer than five people per square mile (fewer than two per sq km).

PEOPLE FROM DIFFERENT LANDS

Today, more than 92 percent of North Dakotans are of European descent. Their ancestors were the immigrants who came to the state in the late 1800s and early 1900s to plow the prairie or raise cattle. Among white North Dakotans, 44 percent trace their roots to Germany and 30 percent to Norway. Many North Dakotans also have

In 1890, 95 percent of North Dakotans lived in rural areas. The state's rural population did not drop below 50 percent until 1990.

Almost 100,000 students attend North Dakota schools each day.

WHAT'S IN A NAME?

The largest natural lake in North Dakota is named Devils Lake. But the Dakota people native to the region call the lake Spirit Lake and call themselves the Spirit Lake Dacotah Nation. Because Europeans once considered Native Americans savage and primitive, they often gave Indian burial sites names that included words like "devil."

ancestors who came from French Canada, Denmark, Finland, Iceland, Poland, and Ukraine.

More than 35,000 Native Americans live in North Dakota, about 60 percent of them on reservations. The most populated reservation is the Turtle Mountain Reservation, which is home to more than 8,000 Ojibwa and Métis people and is located near the Canadian border. Most Hispanics in North Dakota trace their origins to Mexico, while most of the state's Asians come from India, China, the Philippines, Japan, Korea, and Vietnam. African Americans have lived in North Dakota since pioneer times.

EDUCATION

North Dakota has 378 public elementary and high schools and 47 private schools, which serve almost 100,000 students. More than 1,000 other students are taught at home. Everyone between ages 7 and 16 must attend school.

North Dakota's state university system supports 13 colleges and universities. Some people see coal as a fuel of the future. The University of North Dakota at Grand Forks has a renowned coal research laboratory. Students planning on agriculture as a career might choose North Dakota State University at Fargo, which operates the North Dakota Agricultural Experiment Station.

People QuickFacts

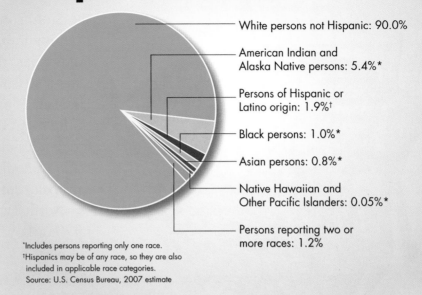

White persons not Hispanic: 90.0%

American Indian and Alaska Native persons: 5.4%*

Persons of Hispanic or Latino origin: 1.9%†

Black persons: 1.0%*

Asian persons: 0.8%*

Native Hawaiian and Other Pacific Islanders: 0.05%*

Persons reporting two or more races: 1.2%

*Includes persons reporting only one race.
†Hispanics may be of any race, so they are also included in applicable race categories.
Source: U.S. Census Bureau, 2007 estimate

Community and religious institutions operate several colleges and universities, including the Roman Catholic University of Mary in Bismarck and the evangelical Trinity Bible College in Ellendale. Sitting Bull College is a tribal college established by the Standing Rock Sioux Tribal Council with the motto, "Let us put our minds together to see what we can build for our children."

ART AND ARTISTS

The scenery along the Upper Missouri River and the Native Americans who lived there inspired some of the greatest paintings of the American West. In the 1830s, George Catlin and Karl Bodmer traveled to North Dakota with sketchbooks and paints to record what they saw.

Catlin, a painter from Pennsylvania, visited about 50 Native American nations, including the Mandan people. He painted portraits of chiefs and scenes of Native American ceremonies. Many of his paintings are in

George Catlin's *Chief of the Mandan Indians and His Wife*

Hidatsa basket

The square dance became the official folk dance of North Dakota in 1995.

the Smithsonian Institution in Washington, D.C. Bodmer, a Swiss artist, painted many landscapes depicting the plains and the Upper Missouri. He also painted Mandans, Hidatsas, and other Native Americans. Catlin's and Bodmer's works provide people today with an idea of how the land and the Native people looked before the arrival of European settlers.

North Dakota today inspires contemporary cowboy artists, such as Walter Piehl Jr. Many of his works show rodeo scenes with bucking horses and roping events. Gary Greff builds gigantic metal sculptures of people and animals on a road outside Regent. Michelle Lindblom paints abstract pictures with acrylics, but she has also painted statues of horses.

The state also claims an accomplished artist who used two names—Ivan Dmitri and Levon West. He was born Levon West and became renowned for his etchings and watercolors, especially *The Spirit of St. Louis*, an etching that shows Charles Lindbergh after he made the first solo airplane flight across the Atlantic Ocean. Later, West became a successful photographer using the name Ivan Dmitri.

Basket weaving was an important skill among Hidatsas, Mandans, and Arikaras. They made baskets for carrying food or firewood by weaving bark onto a frame made from willow sticks. Today, some Native Americans in North Dakota still practice this traditional craft.

North Dakota's Plains Indians decorated their clothing with geometric patterns of colorful glass beads. Beadwork clothing is now rare, but some Native Americans sell beadwork belts, purses, and other items.

LOUISE ERDRICH: NATIVE AMERICAN STORYTELLER

Louise Erdrich (1954—), who was born in Minnesota and raised in Wahpeton, North Dakota, is a storyteller like many of her Ojibwa ancestors. An award-winning poet, novelist, and children's book writer, Erdrich keeps this tradition alive with fascinating stories about Native Americans living along the Red River of the North. Her books include *Love Medicine*, *The Beet Queen*, and *The Plague of Doves*.

 Want to know more? See http://voices.cla.umn.edu/vg/Bios/entries/erdrich_louise.html

Louis L'Amour at his typewriter

Pioneers on the lonely prairie practiced a craft called wheat weaving. They soaked long stalks of wheat in water until they were soft enough to bend and twist. They wove the wheat into many shapes, from figures of cowboys to hearts, angels, and wreaths. Today's North Dakota wheat weavers display their crafts at art fairs.

POETS AND NOVELISTS

The plains and prairies have also inspired North Dakota writers. Louis L'Amour, who was born in Jamestown, wrote 101 books, mostly about the American West. Many of his books were made into hit movies, including *Hondo*, *How the West Was Won*, and *The Quick and the Dead*. Novelist Louise Erdrich, who grew up in Wahpeton, writes books concerned with love, family life, and the difficulties faced by Native Americans

MINI-BIO

PEGGY LEE: COOL JAZZ SINGER

Peggy Lee (1920–2002), who was born in Jamestown, began her singing career on radio station WDAY in Fargo. She joined Benny Goodman's band in 1941. During her long career, Lee made 600 recordings, including hits such as "Fever" and "Is That All There Is?" Her soft, cool voice became known to a generation of kids as the voice of the cocker spaniel, Lady, in Walt Disney's animated film Lady and the Tramp.

Want to know more? See http://governor.nd.gov/awards/rr-gallery/lee.html

living in a white culture. One of the first Native Americans in North Dakota to tell about the ways of her people was Buffalo Bird Woman. She told writer Gilbert L. Wilson Hidatsa stories and about gardening, cooking, and other traditional Hidatsa skills. Wilson interviewed her for 12 years and then wrote two books about her life and Hidatsa philosophy.

North Dakota has its own official poet, Larry Woiwode, who was named poet laureate of the state in 1995. In addition to his poems, which have appeared in many magazines, he has written eight novels.

SPORTS ON THE PRAIRIE

North Dakota does not have any professional sports teams, but the state has produced great athletes. Phil Hansen played football at North Dakota State, and Jim Kleinsasser played at the University of North Dakota before both went on to successful careers in the National Football League. Roger Maris of Fargo knocked a record 61 home runs out of the ballpark during the 1961 baseball season. Maris's record stood for 37 years. Phil Jackson grew up in Williston, played professional basketball, and won lasting acclaim as a coach with the Chicago Bulls and the Los Angles Lakers.

It is no surprise that with its frigid winters, ice hockey is a popular sport with North Dakotans. The state is home to two North American Hockey League teams for young players, the Bismarck Bobcats and the Fargo-Moorhead Jets. Clifford "Fido" Purpur, the first North Dakotan to play on a National Hockey League team, was inducted into the United States Hockey Hall of Fame in 1974.

Roger Maris of Fargo made history in 1961 when he hit 61 home runs for the season.

MINI-BIO

PHIL JACKSON: BASKETBALL'S SUPERCOACH

Phil Jackson (1945–), who grew up in Williston and attended the University of North Dakota, is one of basketball's greatest coaches. Prior to becoming a coach, Jackson proved himself an outstanding defensive player for the New York Knicks and the New Jersey Nets. In 1989, he became head coach of the Chicago Bulls. Building the team around its star player, Michael Jordan, Jackson twice led the Bulls to three championships in a row, for a total of six championships by 1998. He joined the Los Angeles Lakers in 1999 and by 2004 had coached them to three consecutive championships.

? Want to know more? See www.nba.com/coachfile/phil_jackson/

HOW TO TALK LIKE A NORTH DAKOTAN

North Dakotans have some sayings that you are not likely to hear in many other states. If North Dakotans are late for work or school because of a blizzard, they explain that they were "snow stayed." Instead of a snack, they have a "bunny lunch." Some expressions North Dakotans use come from their ancestors. For example, a North Dakotan of Norwegian descent is likely to say "uff-da," instead of "drat" or "good grief!"

HOW TO EAT LIKE A NORTH DAKOTAN

With all the wheat that is grown in North Dakota, it is no surprise that North Dakotans enjoy breads, rolls, and pastas. North Dakotans also enjoy dishes made from the state's plentiful fish and game. They cook up walleye and trout, and they make hamburgers and sausages out of venison. Bison meat from North Dakota buffalo ranches is another favorite. Bison meat tastes much like beef, but contains less fat. In addition, many North Dakotans love some of the recipes that came from Germany and Norway with the immigrants.

Food prepared for the Pitchfork Fondue in Medora

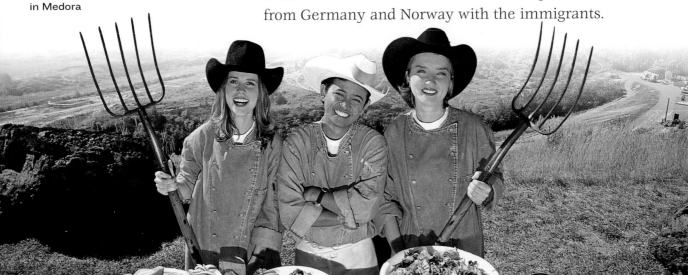

MENU

WHAT'S ON THE MENU IN NORTH DAKOTA?

Chocolate-Covered Potato Chips

North Dakotans love this sweet and salty snack that is made by dipping ridged potato chips into vats of creamy chocolate.

Fleischkuechle

Don't be surprised to see this hard-to-pronounce German dish on the menu. Just say "FLY-shh-keek-la, please," and you will be served tasty deep-fried dumplings stuffed with ground beef.

Norwegian Kumla

Kumla are fat, round dumplings made of grated potatoes mixed with celery and onions.

Kuchen

Kuchen, a German dessert, is like a cross between a cake and a pie. The dough can be topped with all kinds of fruit or custard—or both!

Indian Fry Bread

The bread dough for this Plains Indian dish is fried in oil rather than baked. Some Native Americans add prairie turnips, which grow wild on the Great Plains.

German-Russian Borscht

On cold North Dakota nights, a good, hearty soup will warm you up. The basic ingredients are beets and cabbage, but some cooks add apples, beef, beans, tomatoes, sour cream, yogurt, and all kinds of vegetables.

TRY THIS RECIPE
Puffed Wheat Squares

Every year, North Dakota farmers grow enough wheat to bake 14 billion loaves of bread and serve up almost 4 billion plates of spaghetti. Here's a recipe for making a sweet treat with puffed wheat. Be sure to have an adult nearby to help.

Ingredients:
- ⅓ cup butter or margarine
- ½ cup corn syrup
- 1 cup brown sugar
- 2 tablespoons cocoa powder
- 1 teaspoon vanilla
- 8 cups puffed wheat cereal

Wheat

Instructions:
1. Put the butter or margarine in a large pot and heat over medium-high heat until the butter melts.
2. Add the syrup, sugar, cocoa, and vanilla to the melted butter.
3. Keep heating the mixture until the syrup bubbles.
4. Remove the pot from the burner and add the puffed wheat. Stir until the wheat is coated.
5. Grease a 9" x 12" pan.
6. Spoon the puffed wheat into the pan.
7. Using a spoon coated in butter so that it will not stick to the wheat puffs, press the mixture down to make the top even.
8. Set the pan aside until it is cool.
9. Cut into squares, serve, and enjoy!

Borscht

82

After sixth graders
from Williston
worked to make it
happen, Governor
John Hoeven
signs a bill naming
the chokeberry the
state fruit, 2007.

GOVERNMENT

★

WHY IS IT A GOOD IDEA FOR KIDS IN NORTH DAKOTA TO KNOW ABOUT THEIR STATE GOVERNMENT? Because the government passes laws and provides services that affect kids and their parents. Laws tell how long students must stay in school. The government also collects taxes from families to pay for schools and to build and maintain the roads that school buses travel over. When kids grow up, they have the chance to serve on juries in the courts that make sure the laws are obeyed.

The capitol in Bismarck is sometimes called the Skyscraper on the Prairie.

THE CENTER OF GOVERNMENT

Bismarck has been the capital ever since North Dakota became a state in 1889. The buildings where the state's business is done, however, were built much later. The original capitol, completed in 1884, burned to the ground on a cold December night in 1930. It was replaced by a high-rise more than 241 feet (73 m) tall. The new North Dakota State Capitol Building Tower, nick-named the Skyscraper on the Prairie, was completed in 1934. North Dakota's lawmakers meet in the main building, and the

Capitol Facts

Here are some fascinating facts about North Dakota's state capitol:

Exterior height: 241 feet 8 inches (73.7 m)
Number of floors (including top-floor observation deck): 18
Surrounding park: 132 acres (53 ha)
Completion date: 1934
Cost: About $2 million
Completion date of judicial wing: 1980

Capital City

This map shows places of interest in Bismarck, North Dakota's capital city.

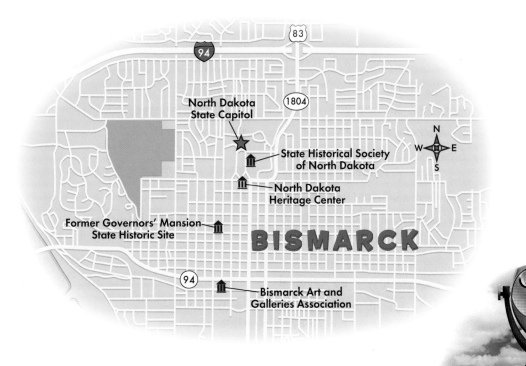

supreme court judges meet in the judicial wing, which was built between 1977 and 1980. The capitol's Hall of Fame honors North Dakotans who have made great contributions in fields from education to entertainment.

The governor lives and works nearby in the Governor's Residence. Built from 1959 to 1960, it has 18 rooms covering more than 10,000 square feet (930 sq m). The first governor's residence, dating from the 1880s, now is home to the State Historical Society of North Dakota. The capitol, the Governor's Residence, the North Dakota Heritage Center, the Liberty Memorial Building (which houses the State Library), and other state office buildings, statues, and memorials are all located in a park called the Capitol Grounds.

SEE IT HERE!

NORTH DAKOTA HERITAGE CENTER

Sharing the Capitol Grounds with the State Capitol and the Governor's Residence is the North Dakota Heritage Center. This museum covers North Dakota's history from prehistoric times to European settlement. Exhibits show the bones of extinct creatures such as mastodons and triceratops that lived in North Dakota long ago. At the museum, you can also see ancient tools, tipis, Red River carts, and displays about the lives of the region's early European settlers.

MINI-BIO

GERALD P. NYE: CRUSADER AGAINST CORRUPTION

Born in Wisconsin, Gerald P. Nye (1892–1971) moved to North Dakota in 1915 and became a newspaper editor and publisher. There he earned the nickname Gerald the Giant-Killer for his investigations into politicians who were corrupted when businesspeople gave them political contributions in exchange for political favors. After he was elected to the U.S. Senate in 1926, Nye headed a committee investigating whether the arms industry had influenced U.S. politicians to enter World War I. He opposed the United States entering World War II, but after the Japanese bombed Pearl Harbor in 1941, he voted for war. Today, Nye is remembered for his strong isolationism and antiwar beliefs.

❓ Want to know more? See http://bioguide.congress.gov/scripts/biodisplay.pl?index=N000176.

North Dakota has the lowest crime rate in the United States.

The state constitution was adopted in 1889, when North Dakota became a state. Since then, it has been amended, or changed, many times. The constitution divides the state government into three separate parts: legislative, executive, and judicial.

THE LEGISLATIVE BRANCH

The North Dakota Legislative Assembly has two parts, a senate and a house of representatives. The state is divided into 47 legislative districts. Voters in each district elect one state senator and two state representatives. The 47 senators and the 94 representatives all serve four-year terms.

The legislature meets only during odd-numbered years. The governor can call the legislature into special session if there are issues that need attention right away. During times when the legislature is not in session, a group called the Legislative Council appoints committees to study issues and make drafts of proposed laws for the next legislative session.

The main job of the legislature is to pass new laws or change existing ones. Either senators or representatives can introduce a proposed law, called a bill. The bill goes to a committee, a small group of legislators

Representative Tony Grindberg speaks to the House Education Committee about a college tuition program in 2007.

who specialize in bills related to specific fields, such as agriculture or taxation. The committee reviews the bill and may make changes, reject the bill, or send it to the full senate or house for a vote. Both the house and the senate must pass a bill before it is sent to the governor to be signed into law.

Legislators may also suggest amendments to the state constitution. If a majority of both the house and the senate vote in favor of an amendment, it then goes before the voters. If a majority of the voters approve it, the amendment passes, and the constitution is changed.

Representing North Dakota

This list shows the number of elected officials who represent North Dakota, both on the state and national levels.

OFFICE	NUMBER	LENGTH OF TERM
State senators	47	4 years
State representatives	94	4 years
U.S. senators	2	6 years
U.S. representatives	1	2 years
Presidential electors	3	—

88

Governor John Hoeven addresses the Commission on Education Improvement in 2006.

WORD TO KNOW

cabinet *a group that advises the head of a government*

THE EXECUTIVE BRANCH

The governor is the head of the executive branch and is elected to a four-year term. Once a bill is passed by the legislature, the governor either can sign the bill into law or can veto, or reject, it. In that case, the legislature may override the veto if it has enough votes. The governor appoints a **cabinet** to help run the state. The cabinet members include commissioners of labor, health, and commerce.

Other elected executive branch officials

PIONEERING PUBLIC OFFICIAL

Laura J. Eisenhuth (1858–1937), who was born in Canada, moved to North Dakota to teach school and in 1892 ran for superintendent of public instruction. She won the election, becoming the first woman in the United States to hold a statewide elected office. After serving only one term, she was defeated for reelection by another woman, Emma F. Bates, who became the second woman in the nation to hold a statewide office.

include the lieutenant governor, who takes over if the governor leaves office or becomes too ill to serve; the attorney general, the leading lawyer for the state who protects the rights and safety of the people; the secretary of state, who oversees elections and keeps track of businesses that operate in North Dakota; and the superintendent of public instruction, who is in charge of the state's public schools. Also elected to serve the state are an agriculture commissioner; an insurance commissioner; and several officials who oversee the state's money, including a treasurer, an auditor, and a tax commissioner. North Dakotans also elect three public service commissioners, who make sure that public services such as electric, gas, and telephone companies serve the people of North Dakota safely and fairly. There is no limit to how many terms elected officials can serve.

The governor, attorney general, and commissioner of agriculture make up the Industrial Commission. The commission oversees the state's oil industry and the state-owned Bank of North Dakota and the North Dakota Mill & Elevator, which were established during the days of the Nonpartisan League.

MINI-BIO

THEODORE ROOSEVELT: TRUST-BUSTING PRESIDENT

Theodore Roosevelt (1858–1919), who served as president from 1901 to 1909, was born and raised in New York City but had a strong connection to North Dakota. He owned cattle ranches in the Badlands of North Dakota, and between 1884 and 1886, he spent many long days riding the range. As president, Roosevelt was a "trust buster," someone who wanted to break up big businesses known as trusts. Examples of trusts were banks, railroads, and the oil industry under the control of big business. To North Dakotans, who often felt cheated by big businesses in other states, Roosevelt was a hero. The state named its award for outstanding citizens the Theodore Roosevelt Rough Rider Award.

? **Want to know more?** See www.whitehouse.gov/history/presidents/tr26.html

WORD TO KNOW

trust *a business that is so large it limits competition*

Tex Hall of the Three Affiliated Tribes speaks at a public hearing about the state water supply.

THE JUDICIAL BRANCH

The highest court in North Dakota is the state supreme court. Its five justices are each elected to 10-year terms. The justices select one of the five to be the chief justice for five years. The supreme court has two jobs. It makes sure that all the courts maintain high standards and operate smoothly. Also, the justices hear **appeals** from people who do not believe

WORD TO KNOW

appeals *legal proceedings in which courts are asked to change the decisions of lower courts*

WEIRD AND WACKY LAWS

North Dakota has some pretty weird laws on the books, but it's safe to say they aren't enforced. Here are a few:

- Don't go dancing in Fargo with a hat on because it is illegal and you could wind up in jail. It is even illegal to wear a hat at a party where other people are dancing.
- If you need to take a nap in North Dakota, take your shoes off. If you lie down and fall asleep with your shoes on, you are breaking the law.
- It is illegal to set off fireworks after 11 P.M. in Devils Lake. (This is probably a good idea on most nights, but what about New Year's Eve?)

North Dakota Government

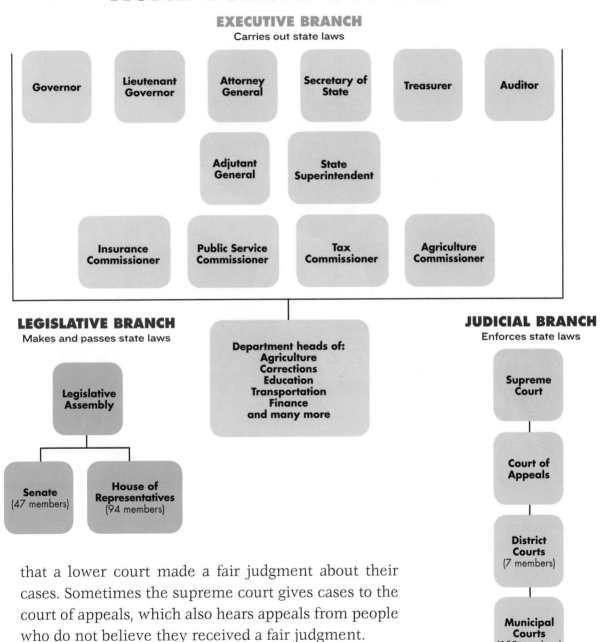

EXECUTIVE BRANCH
Carries out state laws

Governor

Lieutenant Governor

Attorney General

Secretary of State

Treasurer

Auditor

Adjutant General

State Superintendent

Insurance Commissioner

Public Service Commissioner

Tax Commissioner

Agriculture Commissioner

LEGISLATIVE BRANCH
Makes and passes state laws

Legislative Assembly

Senate (47 members)

House of Representatives (94 members)

Department heads of:
Agriculture
Corrections
Education
Transportation
Finance
and many more

JUDICIAL BRANCH
Enforces state laws

Supreme Court

Court of Appeals

District Courts (7 members)

Municipal Courts (100 members)

that a lower court made a fair judgment about their cases. Sometimes the supreme court gives cases to the court of appeals, which also hears appeals from people who do not believe they received a fair judgment.

District courts hear all the civil and criminal cases in the state. Municipal courts handle less important cases such as minor traffic violations and parking tickets.

Voters cast their ballots during the 2008 presidential primaries.

GOVERNMENT CLOSE TO HOME

North Dakota is divided into 53 counties. Each county is governed by a board of commissioners, whose members are elected to four-year terms. North Dakota cities may have one of three types of government—mayor-council, city manager, or board of commissioners. Local governments are in charge of police and fire protection and such services as building and repairing city streets and county roads.

North Dakota Counties

This map shows the 53 counties in North Dakota. Bismarck, the state capital, is indicated with a star.

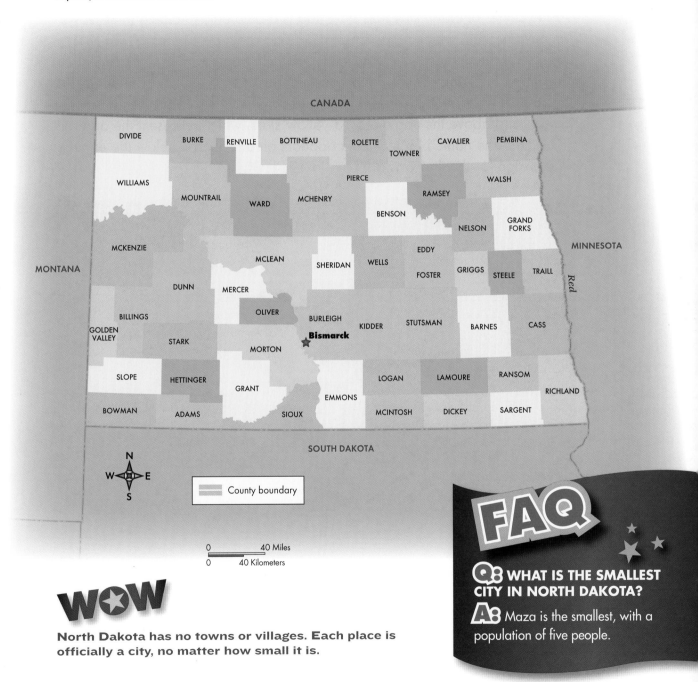

CANADA

DIVIDE · BURKE · RENVILLE · BOTTINEAU · ROLETTE · CAVALIER · PEMBINA

TOWNER

WILLIAMS · MOUNTRAIL · WARD · MCHENRY · PIERCE · RAMSEY · WALSH

BENSON

NELSON · GRAND FORKS

MCKENZIE · MCLEAN · SHERIDAN · WELLS · EDDY · GRIGGS · STEELE · TRAILL

FOSTER

MINNESOTA

DUNN · MERCER · OLIVER · BURLEIGH · KIDDER · STUTSMAN · BARNES · CASS

BILLINGS

GOLDEN VALLEY · STARK · MORTON · **Bismarck** ☆

MONTANA

Red

SLOPE · HETTINGER · GRANT · LOGAN · LAMOURE · RANSOM

RICHLAND

EMMONS

BOWMAN · ADAMS · SIOUX · MCINTOSH · DICKEY · SARGENT

SOUTH DAKOTA

N W E S

County boundary

0 ___ 40 Miles
0 ___ 40 Kilometers

WOW

North Dakota has no towns or villages. Each place is officially a city, no matter how small it is.

FAQ

Q: WHAT IS THE SMALLEST CITY IN NORTH DAKOTA?

A: Maza is the smallest, with a population of five people.

State Flag

At the center of North Dakota's state flag is a bald eagle holding in its claws an olive branch, which represents peace, and a bundle of arrows, which represents the defense of liberty. In its beak, the eagle carries a ribbon with the words *E Pluribus Unum*, which means "Out of Many, One." The eagle has a red, white, and blue shield on its body, which represents the United States, and above the eagle are 13 yellow stars, which represent the original 13 states. The name North Dakota appears on a red scroll below the eagle. The design for the flag was adopted in 1911.

TRACE IT! TRACE IT! TRACE IT!

State Seal

At the center of the seal stands a single oak tree in an open field. To the left of the tree, a Native American on horseback pursues a bison. Bundles of harvested wheat and a farmer's plow stand near the oak tree. A bow and arrows, a sledgehammer, and an anvil are also nearby. The motto "Liberty and Union, Now and Forever, One and Inseparable" arcs over stars, symbolizing North Dakota's being part of the Union. Around the edge of the seal are the words "Great Seal, State of North Dakota," and the date October 1, 1889, when North Dakotans approved the state constitution.

READ ABOUT

A worker at the Sioux Manufacturing Corporation in Fort Totten holds Kevlar, a material used to make protective clothing.

CHAPTER EIGHT

ECONOMY

★

DO YOU LIKE MACARONI AND CHEESE? There's a good chance that the wheat used to make the macaroni pasta came from North Dakota. The fertile soil of the Red River Valley and the sandy soil of the Drift Prairie help put agriculture at the top of North Dakota's economy. Other riches come from North Dakota's land in the form of coal, oil, and natural gas.

Harvesting wheat in Berthold

North Dakota is the nation's number-one producer of honey.

CROPS AND LIVESTOCK

Agriculture is the state's leading business, and wheat is North Dakota's most important crop. In addition to growing more durum and spring wheat than any other state in the nation, North Dakota is the leading producer of navy beans, pinto beans, dry peas, lentils, canola, sunflowers, and barley. In 2006, North Dakota accounted for 94 percent of all the flaxseed produced in the United States. Flaxseed is used to make a range of products from bread to linoleum floor coverings to linseed oil used in oil-based paints. Other crops that are important to the state's economy include sugar beets, potatoes, oats, and corn. Farmers also grow hay to feed North Dakota's livestock herds.

Beef cattle are the most valuable livestock in North Dakota, followed by dairy cows and hogs. North Dakota's ranchers raise enough beef every year to make 113 million hamburgers. Ranchers also raise bison.

Top Products

Agriculture Wheat, barley, flaxseed, canola, dry navy and pinto beans, dry peas, lentils, sunflowers, barley, oats, sugar beets, potatoes, corn, beef cattle, dairy cattle, hogs, sheep, buffalo

Manufacturing Food products, fabricated metal, machinery, electronics

Mining Petroleum, lignite coal, natural gas, sand, gravel, clay

Although most people think of farming when they think of North Dakota, that industry is not as strong as it once was. But farms and ranches still occupy most of the land in the state.

Wheat

ALL KINDS OF SERVICES

Today, many more people work in service industries. These workers do not manufacture a product or grow a crop. Instead, they do things for others. Much of the state's service industry depends on the state's agriculture. For example, people who work in transportation industries drive trucks and trains that carry agricultural products to market. Companies that sell seeds to farmers and banks that give loans to farmers are also service industries.

Many people who work in service industries perform jobs unrelated to agriculture. The auto mechanic who repairs your family car, the dental hygienist who cleans your teeth, and the person who serves your pizza are all service industry workers. Government jobs are a major part of North Dakota's service industry.

The fastest growing part of North Dakota's service industry is tourism. Tour guides, hotel workers, and cooks who rustle up grub for guests at dude ranches are all part of North Dakota's growing tourist industry. By 2006, tourism employed more than 31,000 workers who collectively earned more than $320 million a year.

MINI-BIO

BERTIN C. GAMBLE: RETAIL KING

Bertin C. Gamble (1898–1986) grew up near Arthur, where he met his boyhood pal and future business partner, Phil Skogmo. They moved to Minnesota and created the Gamble-Skogmo retail empire of about 4,200 stores, which included Gambles auto supply, Gambles department stores, Aldens mail order company, Woman's World clothing stores, Red Owl Grocery stores, and Snyder Drug stores. The chain was sold to the Wickes Corporation in 1980, but the Gamble-Skogmo foundation that resulted continues to fund programs for disadvantaged youth, people with disabilities, and low-income senior citizens.

 Want to know more? See www.slphistory.org/history/gambleskogmo.asp

A worker inspects noodles being produced at the Dakota Growers Pasta Company in Carrington.

MAKING THINGS

Food processing is the primary manufacturing industry in North Dakota. Companies in the state make bread and pasta, process and freeze potatoes, and make flaxseed oil, sunflower seed oil, sugar, and milk and cheese products. Meat-processing plants make steaks and sausages from cattle raised in North Dakota's western rangeland.

Other firms in the state make computer and electronics equipment, chemicals, medicines, medical supplies, health-care products, and auto parts. North Dakota has attracted many companies in recent years because it is thought to have a well-educated, industrious workforce. For example, in 2007, Microsoft, the software company

Major Agricultural and Mining Products

This map shows where North Dakota's major agricultural and mining products come from. See a brown cow? That means cattle are raised there.

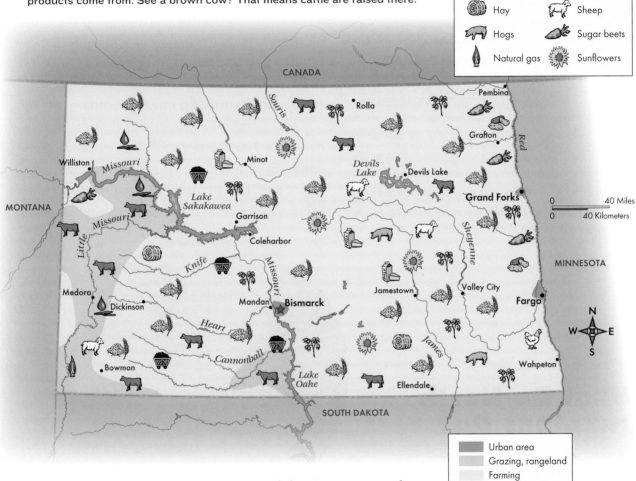

Cattle		Oats	
Coal		Oil	
Dairy		Potatoes	
Grains		Poultry	
Hay		Sheep	
Hogs		Sugar beets	
Natural gas		Sunflowers	

Urban area
Grazing, rangeland
Farming

based in Washington State, announced that it was expanding its operation in Fargo, where it already employed 1,200 people.

THE ENERGY INDUSTRY

A drive west through North Dakota not only takes you to the Badlands and ranch lands, but it also takes you to energy lands. In 2005, five mines in the region

Lying just under the surface in western North Dakota is about **25 billion tons of lignite**, enough to supply the region's coal needs for more than **800 years.**

SEE IT HERE!

GREAT PLAINS SYNFUELS PLANT

Tanks, towers, and pipelines suddenly appear on North Dakota's western prairie, coming together to make up America's only commercial synthetic gas plant, which began operating in 1984. On a tour of the plant, visitors learn how high temperatures and high pressure turn North Dakota's lignite into clean-burning natural gas. A 2-foot (0.6 m) diameter pipe carries the gas from the plant to join other pipelines that bring natural gas to customers all over the West.

produced 30.6 million tons of lignite. Almost 80 percent of the lignite was burned in North Dakota power plants. The state's Industrial Commission supports the Lignite Vision 21 Program to find ways of burning lignite more efficiently and with much less pollution. The program also seeks ways to send more electric power to other states to supply their growing energy needs.

More than 13 percent of lignite mined in North Dakota is processed in the Great Plains Synfuels Plant northwest of Beulah. Every day, this plant turns lignite into clean-burning synthetic natural gas. Many people

What Do North Dakotans Do?

This color-coded chart shows what industries North Dakotans work in.

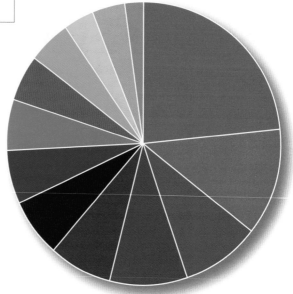

23.4% Educational services, health care, and social assistance, 78,338

12.4% Retail trade, 41,666

9.1% Agriculture, forestry, fishing, hunting, and mining, 30,309

9.0% Arts, entertainment, recreation, accommodation, and food services, 30,174

7.7% Manufacturing, 25,909

6.7% Construction, 22,357

6.1% Professional, scientific, management, administrative, and waste management services, 20,439

5.8% Finance, insurance, real estate, rental, and leasing, 19,410

5.2% Transportation, warehousing, and utilities, 17,435

5.0% Public administration, 16,874

3.7% Other services, except public administration, 12,458

3.7% Wholesale trade, 12,391

2.2% Information, 7,250

Source: U.S. Census Bureau, 2006 estimate

THINK ABOUT IT!

Ethanol Pros and Cons

As gasoline prices soared in the 2000s, scientists and government leaders looked for other sources of energy. One source was ethanol, which is made from plants such as corn and wheat. Mixed with gasoline, ethanol can provide a cleaner-burning fuel for cars, tractors, and trucks. North Dakota's agriculture commissioner Roger Johnson testified, "Ethanol is a **renewable**, domestic source of fuel. We should be producing and using more of it to lessen our dependence on foreign oil."

Not everyone supports the use of ethanol, however. Professor Tad W. Patzek of the University of California–Berkeley points out that making ethanol uses more energy than the ethanol produces. "In terms of renewable fuels, ethanol is the worst solution," he says. "It has the highest energy cost with the least benefit."

Others believe that using crop plants for fuel drives up the cost of food. "We're putting the supermarket in competition with the corner filling station for the output of the farm," said Lester R. Brown, president of the Earth Policy Institute.

believe that such innovative production of energy is what the United States needs to decrease its use of oil from foreign countries.

North Dakota has another great energy resource in the form of petroleum. No one is sure how much oil could be pumped from the rocks under North Dakota. Some experts estimate it to be about 200 billion barrels.

Another resource that North Dakota has is wind. Energy companies are beginning to harness the wind on the prairies. In south-central North Dakota, 41 wind **turbines** produce enough electricity to supply 19,000 homes.

Energy also comes from corn. Some corn is being turned into ethanol, a fuel for automobiles. North Dakota farmers grew more than 160 million bushels of corn in 2006, and much of it was used to produce more than 50 million gallons (189 million liters) of ethanol.

WORDS TO KNOW

renewable *referring to an energy source such as wind, water, or plants that cannot be used up*

turbines *machines that make power through the rotation of blades powered by wind, water, or steam*

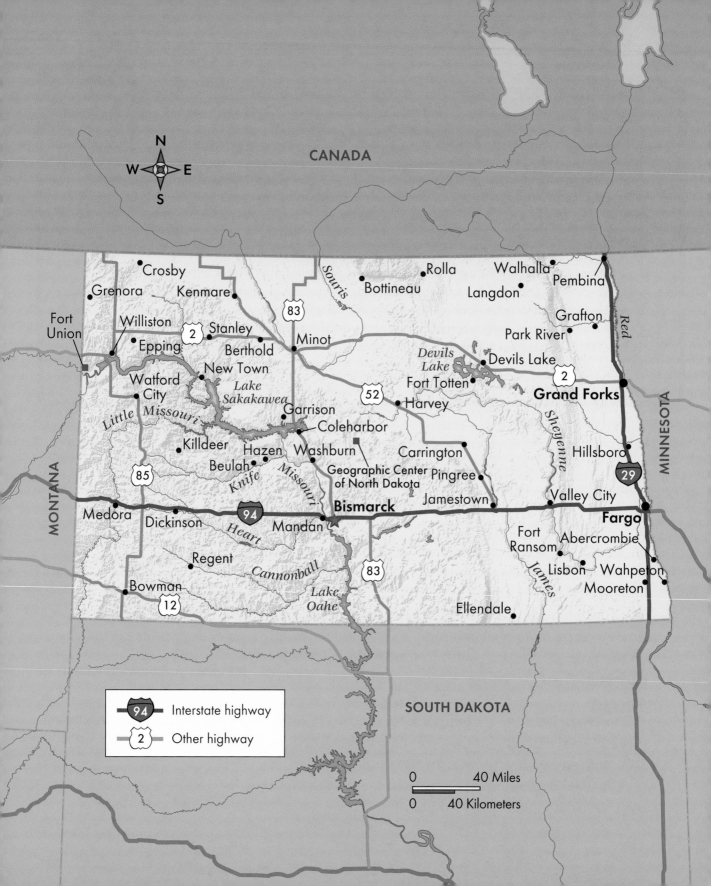

CHAPTER NINE

TRAVEL GUIDE

★

IF YOU WANT TO SEE REMINDERS OF THE OLD WEST, TAKE A DRIVE ACROSS NORTH DAKOTA. Fields of golden wheat now grow on grasslands where the bison roamed. You can still see herds of bison, however, on ranches and game preserves. Along the Missouri River, you can stop at forts used by the U.S. cavalry or visit replicas of earth lodges and tipis that the Native Americans called home.

← Follow along with this travel map. We'll start our trip in Bowman and end in Walhalla.

TRAVEL GUIDE TRAVEL GUIDE

WEST

THINGS TO DO: Go bird-watching, step inside a homesteader's log cabin, and ride a horse through the colorful, crumbling hillsides in the Badlands.

Bowman

★ **Pioneer Trails Regional Museum:** Travel through time in this museum as you view displays devoted to dinosaurs, Native American cultures, homesteaders, and cowboys. There's also a re-creation of a sod house literally cut from the prairie.

Coleharbor

★ **Audubon National Wildlife Refuge:** If you enjoy bird-watching, head for this refuge on Lake Audubon.

Audubon National Wildlife Refuge

Dakota Dinosaur Museum

Dickinson

★ **Dakota Dinosaur Museum:** Yes, dinosaurs did live in North Dakota, and here you can see replicas of *Allosaurus, Albertosaurus, Thescelosaurus*, and *Stegosaurus*.

Crosby

★ **Divide County Museum:** This far northwest county of North Dakota contains a pioneer village of about 25 historic buildings, including a bank and general store.

Epping

★ **Downtown Epping:** Seven historic buildings have been transformed into the Buffalo Trails Museum. Here you can imagine how the homesteaders lived in a log cabin, cringe at the thought of a visit to the dentist's office, and relive school days in the original Stevens country school.

Grenora

★ **Writing Rock State Historic Site:** Take a picnic lunch to this spot where long ago Native American artists carved images of thunderbirds—mythical creatures sacred to them—into two granite boulders.

Kenmare

★ **Danish Mill:** Built in 1902 by a Danish immigrant, this windmill was a place where local farmers ground their spring wheat into flour. In 1959, the mill was moved into a park in town and then restored. Today, you can tour the mill and see how it worked.

Horseback riding in the Badlands

Killdeer

★ **Little Missouri State Park:** Wind and water have eroded the rocks in this region of the Badlands into fantastic shapes. You can see them only by walking or riding a horse along some of the park's 30 miles (48 km) of trails.

Medora

★ **Old Town Hall Theater:** Watch *Bully*, a play about former U.S. president Theodore Roosevelt. Taking its name from his favorite expression—"Bully!"—the play runs from May through August.

★ **Burning Hills Amphitheatre:** Enjoy *Medora Musical*, a two-hour outdoor country-and-western performance in this restored historic town.

Medora Musical

MINI-BIO

MARQUIS DE MORES: ROMANTIC RANCHER

One of North Dakota's most colorful early ranchers was a restless French nobleman born in Paris, the Marquis de Mores (1858–1896). He moved to North Dakota to become a cattle rancher after a brief career in the French military. He founded the town of Medora, which he named for his wife, and built a meatpacking plant there. De Mores had a hot temper and fought several duels. After a bad winter wiped out his cattle, and his meatpacking plant failed, he returned to France. He was involved in many more adventures, including a plan to force the British to leave North Africa, where he was eventually murdered.

? Want to know more? See www.theodorerooseveltcenter.com/DeMores.asp

Mountain biking on Maah Daah Hey Trail

★ **Chateau de Mores State Historic Site:** The central attraction in this park is the Chateau de Mores, a 26-room summer home built in 1883 by the Marquis de Mores, a wealthy Frenchman and rancher.

★ **North Dakota Cowboy Hall of Fame:** Learn about ranching, rodeo, and life in the Badlands.

★ **Maah Daah Hey Trail:** You can hike, ride a horse, or mountain bike along this 96-mile (154 km) trail that connects the north and south sections of Theodore Roosevelt National Park. The name comes from a Mandan phrase that means "area that has been around for a long time."

Stanley

★ **Flickertail Village Museum:**
Tour 18 buildings to get an idea
of how pioneers lived in Stanley's
early days. The buildings include
a jail, school, church, and country
store. You can also see dolls that
pioneer girls once played with.

**Salem Sue, the world's largest
cow, stands on a hill in New
Salem. She measures 38 feet
(11.5 m) high and 50 feet (15 m)
long. Made of fiberglass, Sue
can be seen for miles around.**

Regent

★ **Enchanted Highway:** Take Exit
72 off of Interstate 94 and follow
the road south to see a fascinating
collection of giant sculptures, with
names such as *Pheasants on the
Prairie*, made by artist Gary Greff.

Pheasants on the Prairie, Enchanted Highway

SEE IT HERE!

FORT UNION

Step through the huge wooden gates of Fort Union
Trading Post National Historic Site in Williston to see
people in costumes typical of the 1800s carrying
on activities typical of the western frontier, such as
blacksmithing and trading furs. The post was built in
1828 by the American Fur Company. Native Americans
visited it to trade furs and bison robes for guns and
other supplies. The army tore down the fort and used
the materials to build Fort Buford, but a replica was built
in the 1980s and 1990s.

Williston

★ **Fort Buford State Historic Site:**
Built in 1866, the fort is remembered as the place where the great
Lakota chief Sitting Bull surren-
dered. The army abandoned the
fort in 1895, and today just three
buildings remain standing—a stone
powder magazine (where gunpow-
der was stored), officers' quarters,
and a guard building.

★ **Missouri-Yellowstone Confluence Interpretive Center:** Here you can learn about the geology, geography, and history of the area where two important rivers meet. You can also view murals and exhibits that tell about the Lewis and Clark expedition.

CENTRAL

THINGS TO DO: Admire the work of some of the state's best artists, thrill to a live rodeo, and relax on a riverboat cruise.

Bismarck

★ **Buckstop Junction:** See a railroad depot, bank, hotel, barbershop, and other buildings dating from 1875 to 1935. They're all on this site on the Missouri Valley Fairgrounds.

A 1907 Northern Pacific caboose at Buckstop Junction

Former Governors' Mansion

★ **Former Governors' Mansion:** Tour the Victorian mansion where North Dakota's governors and their families lived from 1893 to 1960. The mansion was built in 1884 as a private home, and the state bought it for $5,000 in 1893. After acquiring the building in 1975, the State Historical Society of North Dakota restored it to look as it did in 1893.

★ **Bismarck Art & Galleries Association:** This center for fine arts hosts exhibits of paintings, photographs, and sculptures. You can also take some classes here.

★ **Bismarck Civic Center:** This site hosts all kinds of events, from rodeo competitions to basketball games to ballets.

★ **Dakota Zoo:** Bismarck's Dakota Zoo grew from a farm where the family loved animals into a full-fledged, self-supporting zoo that opened to the public in 1961.

★ **Lewis and Clark Riverboat:** Climb aboard this 150-passenger riverboat for a daytime or sunset cruise on the Upper Missouri River and get a feel for the historic river journey taken by Lewis and Clark.

★ **Gateway to Science Center:** Kids love this museum, where the rocket in a bottle, magnetic motion, optical illusions, human kaleidoscope, and other hands-on activities bring science to life.

Mandan

★ **Dacotah Speedway:** Head to this track for auto races and demolition derbies.

On-a-Slant Village

SEE IT HERE!

WHERE CUSTER SLEPT

You can experience the world of General George Armstrong Custer and the Seventh U.S. Cavalry at the reconstructed historic Fort Abraham Lincoln and at the house where Custer lived from 1873 to 1876. Custer and his soldiers headed out in 1876 to the fateful meeting with Lakotas, led by Sitting Bull and Crazy Horse, at the Battle of the Little Bighorn, in which Custer and many of his men died. Today, guides wearing the blue coats of soldiers or the dresses of laundry women take you on a living history tour.

★ **On-a-Slant Village:** Here you can learn the history of the Native American people who lived in a village on the sloping banks of the Missouri River. Guides tell the history and lifestyle of the Mandan as you visit the site's five reproductions of earth lodges.

Raging Rivers Water Park

★ **Raging Rivers Water Park:** When the hot summer days get to you, head here to cool off. Zip down a waterslide or just lie back in a tube and float down the Lazy River.

Devils Lake/Fort Totten

★ **Fort Totten State Historic Site:** Fort Totten is the best-preserved historic site in North Dakota. Built as a military post in 1867, the fort became a boarding school for Native American children in 1890, and in 1960 it became a state historic site.

Jamestown

★ **National Buffalo Museum:** You can see paintings, bison bones, and Native American artwork all centered on the history and importance of bison.

★ **Stutsman County Memorial Museum:** Located in a former pioneer mansion, this museum has a range of displays that include period rooms from the late 1800s and early 1900s, a post office, railroad artifacts, and local wildlife.

Pingree

★ **Arrowwood National Wildlife Refuge Complex Headquarters:** This complex of six wildlife projects covers 5.5 million acres (2.2 million ha) and is a great place to watch and photograph wildlife.

North Dakota has 63 national wildlife refuges, more than any other state.

Washburn

★ **McLean County Historical Society Museums:** Exhibits in this series of museums cover everything from fossils to area wildlife and pioneer home life.

Minot

★ **Splashdown Dakota Super Slides:** Who cares if it's snowing outside? You can still have fun in the water at North Dakota's first indoor water park.

★ **Norsk Høstfest:** North America's largest Scandinavian Festival, this annual event celebrating North Dakota's Scandinavian heritage takes place in late September or early October, with food, crafts, and entertainment.

EAST

THINGS TO DO: Eat, dance, and sing at a German folk festival, go canoeing or hiking, or take a spin on an antique carousel.

Fargo

★ **Fargo Air Museum:** About a dozen historic aircraft, mainly from the World War II era, are on display at this museum.

Fargo Air Museum

Plains Art Museum

★ **Plains Art Museum:** See paintings, photographs, and sculptures that feature Native American artists and touch on themes that reflect the land and people of North Dakota.

★ **German Folk Festival:** Every July, you can enjoy German food, view German crafts, and listen to a German band at the Rheault Farm, a 15-acre (6 ha) park owned by the Fargo Park District.

★ **Red River Zoo:** View animals that live in climates similar to that of Fargo. You might be surprised to find a Bactrian camel, a red panda, and a Persian onager.

★ **Thunder Road Fun Park:** Ride bumper cars, race go-carts, hit a few balls in the batting cage, or play miniature golf at this amusement park designed for family fun.

Mooreton

★ **Bagg Bonanza Farm National Historic Landmark:** This once-thriving 9,000-acre (3,600 ha) wheat farm shut down in 1950. The restored farmhouse, bunkhouse, and other buildings are now an antique-filled museum.

★ **Pembina State Museum:** This museum traces the area's rich history, with exhibits of fossils from ancient Lake Agassiz, stone and bone tools made by early people, and artifacts from Native Americans, fur traders, and railroad builders.

Fort Ransom

★ **Fort Ransom State Park:** Here you can rent a canoe or kayak and take a trip along the Sheyenne River. In the winter, you can cross-country ski or snowmobile along the park's scenic trails.

Fort Ransom State Park

Bagg Bonanza Farm National Historic Landmark

Grand Forks

★ **The Greenway:** On about 2,200 acres (890 ha) of open space in the heart of the city, you can camp, golf, hike, or fish. You can also enjoy special events during the year, such as the Greenway Ski Days in February, featuring cross-country skiing and sleigh rides.

★ **Splasher's of the South Seas:** Pretend you are in the tropics as a huge bucket of water splashes down on the pool like a tropical rainstorm at the largest indoor water park in the state.

★ **North Dakota Museum of Art:** This is the state's official museum of art. Located on the University of North Dakota campus, it houses exhibits of regional, national, and international art.

SEE IT HERE!

INTERNATIONAL PEACE GARDEN

Straddling the border of North Dakota and Manitoba, this formal garden is a symbol of friendship between Canada and the United States. The gardens contain the Peace Chapel and the Peace Tower. In summer, some 15,000 flowers create patterns such as the floral clock and floral flag designs of both countries. The gardens inspired North Dakota's nickname, Peace Garden State.

Abercrombie

★ **Fort Abercrombie State Historic Site:** Built in 1858 to protect steamboats on the Red River and carts on the Pembina Trail, this was the first fort in what became North Dakota.

Prairie Rose Carousel

Wahpeton

★ **Prairie Rose Carousel:** Climb up on one of the 20 carefully restored wooden horses or just sit in one of two fancy chariots for a ride on an antique carousel dating from 1926.

Walhalla

★ **Gingras State Historic Site:** The two oldest buildings in North Dakota that are still standing are located at this Red River Valley fur-trading post built in the 1840s. Antoine B. Gingras, a trader, constructed a rough log building for trading and a clapboard-sided log building, painted red, for his house.

WRITING PROJECTS

Check out these ideas for creating a campaign brochure and writing you-are-there narratives. Or you can research the lives of famous people from North Dakota.

118

ART PROJECTS

You can illustrate the state song, create a dazzling PowerPoint presentation, or learn about the state quarter and design your own.

119

TIMELINE

What happened when? This timeline highlights important events in the state's history—and shows what was happening throughout the United States at the same time.

122

FAST FACTS

Use this section to find fascinating facts about state symbols, land area and population statistics, weather, sports teams, and much more.

126

GLOSSARY

Remember the Words to Know from the chapters in this book? They're all collected here.

125

SCIENCE, TECHNOLOGY, & MATH PROJECTS

Make weather maps, graph population statistics, and research endangered species that live in the state.

120

PRIMARY VS. SECONDARY SOURCES

121

So what are primary and secondary sources? And what's the diff? This section explains all that and where you can find them.

BIOGRAPHICAL DICTIONARY

133

This at-a-glance guide highlights some of the state's most important and influential people. Visit this section and read about their contributions to the state, the country, and the world.

RESOURCES

Books, Web sites, DVDs, and more. Take a look at these additional sources for information about the state.

137

WRITING PROJECTS

★ ★ ★

Write a Memoir, Journal, or Editorial for Your School Newspaper!

Picture Yourself . . .

★ As part of a Mandan family, living in a snug earth lodge with a fire pit in the center. You are sitting with your brothers and sisters beside the fire pit on a mat of woven bulrushes. What is life like? Describe the sights, sounds, smells, and tastes of your world.

SEE: Chapter Two, pages 27–28.

GO TO: www.pbs.org/lewisandclark/native/man.html

★ As an American settler living on the North Dakota frontier. What hardships would you face as you tried to build a new life in North Dakota?

SEE: Chapter Four, pages 47–52.

GO TO: www.museumoftheamericanwest.org/explore/exhibits/sod/daily.html

Create an Election Brochure or Web Site!

Run for office! Throughout this book, you've read about some of the issues that concern North Dakota today. As a candidate for governor of North Dakota, create a campaign brochure or Web site.

★ Explain how you meet the qualifications to be governor of North Dakota.

★ Talk about the three or four major issues you'll focus on if you're elected.

★ Remember, you'll be responsible for North Dakota's budget. How would you spend the taxpayers' money?

SEE: Chapter Seven, pages 88–89.

GO TO: North Dakota's Government Web site at www.nd.gov. You might also want to read some local newspapers. Try these:

Bismarck Tribune at www.bismarcktribune.com

Forum (Fargo) at www.in-forum.com

Create an interview script with a famous person from North Dakota!

★ Research various North Dakotans, such as Sitting Bull, Woody Keeble, Louise Erdrich, Peggy Lee, Roger Maris, Phil Jackson, and Theodore Roosevelt.

★ Based on your research, pick one person you would most like to talk with.

★ Write a script of the interview. What questions would you ask? How would this person answer? Create a question-and-answer format. You may want to supplement this writing project with a voice-recording dramatization of the interview.

SEE: Chapters Four, Five, Six, and Seven, pages 53, 64, 77, 78, 79, and 89, and the Biographical Dictionary, pages 133–136.

GO TO: http://governor.nd.gov/awards/rr-gallery/toc.html

ART PROJECTS

★　★　★

Create a PowerPoint Presentation or Visitors' Guide

Welcome to North Dakota!

North Dakota's a great place to visit and to live! From its natural beauty to its historical sites, there's plenty to see and do. In your PowerPoint presentation or brochure, highlight 10 to 15 of North Dakota's fascinating landmarks. Be sure to include:

★ a map of the state showing where these sites are located

★ photos, illustrations, Web links, natural history facts, geographic stats, climate and weather, plants and wildlife, and recent discoveries

SEE: Chapter Nine, pages 104–115, and Fast Facts, pages 126–127.

GO TO: The official tourism Web site for North Dakota at www.ndtourism.com. Download and print maps, photos, and vacation ideas for tourists.

Illustrate the Lyrics to the North Dakota State Song

("North Dakota Hymn")

Use markers, paints, photos, collages, colored pencils, or computer graphics to illustrate the lyrics to "North Dakota Hymn." Turn your illustrations into a picture book, or scan them into PowerPoint and add music.

SEE: The lyrics to "North Dakota Hymn" on page 128.

GO TO: The North Dakota state government Web site at www.nd.gov to find out more about the origin of the state song.

State Quarter Project

From 1999 to 2008, the U.S. Mint introduced new quarters commemorating each of the 50 states in the order that they were admitted to the Union. Each state's quarter features a unique design on its back, or reverse.

GO TO: www.usmint.gov/kids and find out what's featured on the back of the North Dakota quarter.

★ Research the significance of the image. Who designed the quarter? Who chose the final design?

★ Design your own North Dakota quarter. What images would you choose for the reverse?

★ Make a poster showing the North Dakota quarter and label each image.

SCIENCE, TECHNOLOGY, & MATH PROJECTS

★ ★ ★

Graph Population Statistics!

★ Compare population statistics (such as ethnic background, birth, death, and literacy rates) in North Dakota counties or major cities. In your graph or chart, look at population density and write sentences describing what the population statistics show; graph one set of population statistics and write a paragraph explaining what the graphs reveal.

SEE: Chapter Six, pages 72–75.

GO TO: The official Web site for the U.S. Census Bureau at www.census.gov and at http://quickfacts.census.gov/qfd/states/38000.html, to find out more about population statistics, how they work, and what the statistics are for North Dakota.

Create a Weather Map of North Dakota!

Use your knowledge of North Dakota's geography to research and identify conditions that result in specific weather events. What is it about the geography of North Dakota that makes it vulnerable to droughts or tornadoes? Create a weather map or poster that shows the weather patterns over the state. Include a caption explaining the technology used to measure weather phenomena and provide data.

SEE: Chapter One, pages 14–15.

GO TO: Visit the National Oceanic and Atmospheric Administration's National Weather Service Web site at www.weather.gov for weather maps and forecasts for North Dakota.

Gray wolf

Track Endangered Species

Using your knowledge of North Dakota's wildlife, research which animals and plants are endangered or threatened.

★ Find out what the state is doing to protect these species.

★ Chart known populations of the animals and plants, and report on changes in certain geographic areas.

SEE: Chapter One, page 19.

GO TO: Web sites such as www.fws.gov/northdakotafieldoffice/endspecies/endangered_species.htm for lists of endangered species in North Dakota.

PRIMARY VS. SECONDARY SOURCES

★ ★ ★

What's the Diff?

Your teacher may require at least one or two primary sources and one or two secondary sources for your assignment. So, what's the difference between the two?

★ **Primary sources are original.** You are reading the actual words of someone's diary, journal, letter, autobiography, or interview. Primary sources can also be photographs, maps, prints, cartoons, news/film footage, posters, first-person newspaper articles, drawings, musical scores, and recordings. By the way, when you conduct a survey, interview someone, shoot a video, or take photographs to include in a project, you are creating primary sources!

★ **Secondary sources are what you find in encyclopedias, textbooks, articles, biographies, and almanacs.** These are written by a person or group of people who tell about something that happened to someone else. Secondary sources also recount what another person said or did. This book is an example of a secondary source.

Now that you know what primary sources are—where can you find them?

★ **Your school or local library:** Check the library catalog for collections of original writings, government documents, musical scores, and so on. Some of this material may be stored on microfilm. The Library of Congress Web site (www.loc.gov) is an excellent online resource for primary source materials.

★ **Historical societies:** These organizations keep historical documents, photographs, and other materials. Staff members can help you find what you are looking for. History museums are also great places to see primary sources firsthand.

★ **The Internet:** There are lots of sites that have primary sources you can download and use in a project or assignment.

TIMELINE

★ ★ ★

U.S. Events | **c. 500 BCE** | **North Dakota Events**

c. 500 BCE
The Woodland period begins.

c. 100 BCE

c. 100 BCE
People in North Dakota begin trading with people to the south and the east.

c. 500 CE

c. 500 CE
People in North Dakota begin using bows and arrows.

c. 800

c. 800
People in North Dakota begin planting corn.

1600

Quiver of arrows

1607
The first permanent English settlement in North America is established at Jamestown.

c. 1600
Dakota groups begin moving west.

1700

1738
The first Europeans reach today's North Dakota.

Mid-1700s
Plains Indians acquire horses.

1776
Thirteen American colonies declare their independence from Great Britain.

1780s
The fur trade begins along the Upper Missouri River.

1787
The U.S. Constitution is written.

Lewis and Clark with Sacagawea

1800

1803
The Louisiana Purchase almost doubles the size of the United States.

1804–05
Lewis and Clark spend the winter at Fort Mandan.

1812–15
The United States and Great Britain fight the War of 1812.

U.S. Events

1830
The Indian Removal Act forces eastern Native American groups to relocate west of the Mississippi River.

1861-65
The American Civil War is fought between the Northern Union and the Southern Confederacy.

Building the Northern Pacific Railway

1886
Apache leader Geronimo surrenders to the U.S. Army, ending the last major Native American rebellion against the expansion of the United States into the West.

1898
The United States gains control of Cuba, Puerto Rico, the Philippines, and Guam after defeating Spain in the Spanish-American War.

1917-18
The United States engages in World War I.

1920
The Nineteenth Amendment to the U.S. Constitution grants women the right to vote.

North Dakota Events

1818
The first school in North Dakota opens at Pembina.

c. 1850
Métis invent Red River carts to carry goods on the Pembina Trail to Minnesota.

1861
The United States creates the Dakota Territory.

1873
The first railroad across North Dakota reaches the Missouri River.

1874-76
Sitting Bull and other Lakotas resist being forced onto reservations.

1880s
Theodore Roosevelt establishes ranches in the Badlands.

1886-87
Blizzards destroy cattle herds in the Badlands.

1889
North Dakota becomes the 39th state.

1900

1915
The Nonpartisan League is founded.

1919
State-owned businesses are established.

U.S. Events

1929

The stock market crashes, plunging the United States more deeply into the Great Depression.

1941–45

The United States engages in World War II.

1951–53

The United States engages in the Korean War.

1964–73

The United States engages in the Vietnam War.

1991

The United States and other nations engage in the brief Persian Gulf War against Iraq.

2000

2001

Terrorists attack the United States on September 11.

2003

The United States and coalition forces invade Iraq.

2008

The United States elects its first African American president, Barack Obama.

North Dakota Events

1930s

Severe drought strikes the Great Plains.

1941–45

Lakota and Dakota code talkers help win World War II.

1947

Construction begins on Garrison Dam.

1951

Oil is discovered near Tioga.

1956

The Nonpartisan League joins the state Democratic Party.

1960s

The lignite mining industry grows.

1984

A plant opens to convert lignite to natural gas.

An oil well in Tioga

2007

Oil companies begin drilling in western North Dakota.

GLOSSARY

acid rain pollution that falls to the earth in raindrops

appeals legal proceedings in which courts are asked to change the decisions of lower courts

archaeologists people who study the remains of past human societies

cabinet a group that advises the head of a government

cavalry soldiers who fight on horseback

corps a group working together on a special mission

endangered at risk of becoming extinct

ethanol an alcohol used as a gasoline substitute, made by fermenting corn or other material

expedition a trip for the purpose of exploration

foreclosed took back property because payment was overdue

isolationists people who believe that their country should not become involved with the problems of foreign nations

lignite a soft type of coal that does not produce as much energy as hard coal

prejudice an unreasonable hatred or fear of others based on race, religion, ethnic group, gender, or other factors

prospectors people who explore a region searching for valuable minerals

recall a vote to remove elected officials from office

receded pulled or moved back over time

renewable referring to an energy source such as wind, water, or plants that cannot be used up

reservoir artificial lake or tank for storing water

sediment material eroded from rocks and deposited elsewhere by wind, water, or glaciers

semiarid receiving 10 to 20 inches (25 to 51 cm) of rain every year

Socialist Party a political group that favors socialism, a political system based on shared or governmental ownership of the production and distribution of goods

sod soil thickly packed together with grass and roots

stocks shares in the ownership of a company

strip mines places where soil or rock is scraped from the earth's surface to reach coal or ores

synthetic related to something that doesn't occur in nature

threatened likely to become endangered in the foreseeable future

trust a business that is so large it limits competition

turbines machines that make power through the rotation of blades powered by wind, water, or steam

FAST FACTS

★ ★ ★

State Symbols

Statehood date	November 2, 1889, the 39th state
Origin of state name	*Dakota* is Sioux for "friend" or "ally"
State capital	Bismarck
State nicknames	Peace Garden State, Sioux State, Flickertail State
State motto	"Liberty and Union, Now and Forever, One and Inseparable"
State bird	Western meadowlark
State flower	Wild prairie rose
State fish	Northern pike
State grass	Western wheatgrass
State fossil	Teredo petrified wood
State song	"North Dakota Hymn"
State tree	American elm
State fair	Third week in July at Minot

State seal

Geography

Total area; rank	70,700 square miles (183,112 sq km); 19th
Land; rank	68,976 square miles (178,647 sq km); 17th
Water; rank	1,724 square miles (4,465 sq km), 22nd
Inland water; rank	1,724 square miles (4,465 sq km), 12th
Geographic center	Sheridan, 5 miles (8 km) southwest of McClusky
Latitude	45°55' N to 49° N
Longitude	97° W to 104° W
Highest point	White Butte, 3,506 feet (1,069 m), located in Slope County
Lowest point	Red River of the North at 750 feet (229 m), located in Pembina County
Largest city	Fargo
Number of counties	53
Longest river	Red River of the North

Population

Population; rank (2007 estimate)	639,715; 48th
Density (2007 estimate)	9 persons per square mile (3 per sq km)
Population distribution (2000 census)	56% urban, 44% rural
Race (2007 estimate)	White persons: 91.6%*
	American Indian and Alaska Native persons: 5.4%*
	Black persons: 1.0%*
	Asian persons: 0.8%*
	Native Hawaiian and Other Pacific Islanders: 0.05%*
	Persons reporting two or more races: 1.2%
	Persons of Hispanic or Latino origin: 1.9%†
	White persons not Hispanic: 90.0%

Includes persons reporting only one race.
†*Hispanics may be of any race, so they are also included in applicable race categories.*

Weather

Record high temperature	121°F (49°C) at Steele on July 6, 1936
Record low temperature	−60°F (−51°C) at Parshall on February 15, 1936
Average July temperature	70°F (21°C)
Average January temperature	10°F (−12°C)
Average yearly precipitation	16 inches (41 cm)

State flag

STATE SONG

★ ★ ★

"North Dakota Hymn"

In 1926, Minnie J. Nielson, the North Dakota superintendent of public instruction, asked poet James Foley of Bismarck to write the lyrics for a song about North Dakota. He created a poem that could be sung to the tune of the "Austrian Hymn," which had music by C. S. Putnam. The first public performance of "North Dakota Hymn" was in the Bismarck City Auditorium in 1927.

North Dakota, North Dakota,
With thy prairies wide and free,
All thy sons and daughters love thee.
Fairest state from sea to sea,
North Dakota, North Dakota,
Here we pledge ourselves to thee.
North Dakota, North Dakota,
Here we pledge ourselves to thee.

Hear thy loyal children singing,
Songs of happiness and praise,
Far and long the echoes ringing
Through the vastness of thy ways—
North Dakota, North Dakota,
We will serve thee all our days.
North Dakota, North Dakota,
We will serve thee all our days.

NATURAL AREAS AND HISTORIC SITES

★ ★ ★

National Park

Theodore Roosevelt National Park preserves the North Dakota Badlands and honors the memory of the 26th president, a great conservationist.

National Scenic Trail

The *North Country National Scenic Trail* is a 4,000-mile (6,400 km) route that traverses woods, prairies, and mountains. This national scenic trail passes through North Dakota and six other northern states.

National Historic Sites

Fort Union Trading Post National Historic Site is a 19th-century trading post where Assiniboines, Crows, Crees, Ojibwas, Blackfeet, Hidatsas, and others brought furs to exchange for other goods.

The *Knife River Indian Villages National Historic Site* features a reconstructed earth lodge, ceremonial clothing, and tools used by Native people a thousand years ago.

National Historic Trail

The *Lewis & Clark National Historic Trail* passes through part of North Dakota, following the route of Lewis and Clark's journey.

State Parks

North Dakota's state park system features and maintains 21 state parks and recreation areas, including *Beaver Lake State Park*, *Devils Lake State Park*, and *Fort Abraham Lincoln State Park*, which is home to On-a-Slant Village and George Armstrong Custer's house.

Mandan earth lodges at On-a-Slant Village

SPORTS TEAMS

★ ★ ★

NCAA Teams (Division I)

North Dakota State University *Bison*
University of North Dakota *Fighting Sioux*

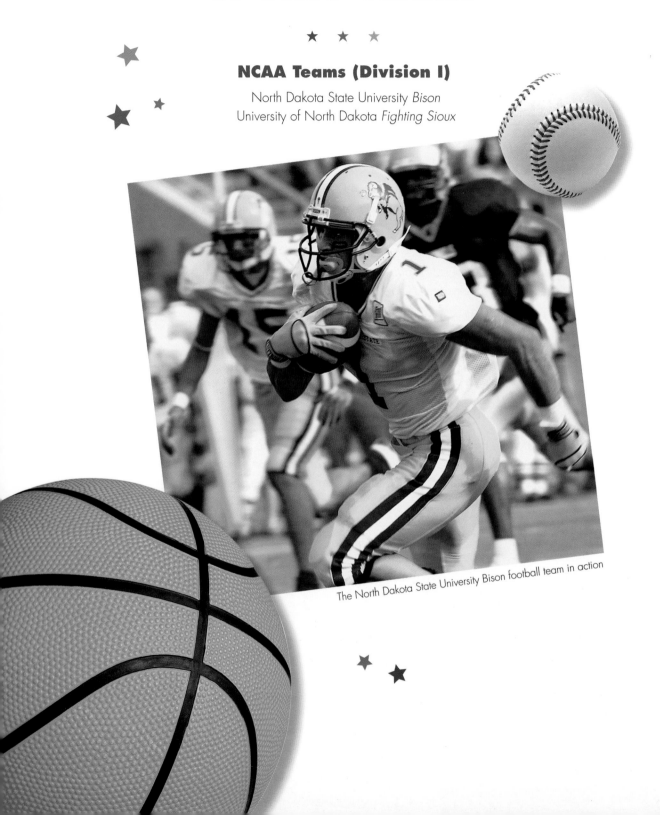

The North Dakota State University Bison football team in action

CULTURAL INSTITUTIONS

Libraries

The *University of North Dakota* (Grand Forks) has a complete set of the papers of the Nuremberg War Crimes Trial, which document World War II war crimes. It also holds a fine collection on the state's history.

North Dakota State University (Fargo) has one of the state's largest libraries and also houses a fine collection on North Dakota history.

The *State Historical Society* (Bismarck) has collections on the state's early history.

Museums

The *Gateway to Science Center* (Bismarck) is an interactive museum about science.

The *Geographical Center Pioneer Village and Museum* (Rugby) is located near the geographic center of North America.

The *North Dakota Heritage Center* (Bismarck) has displays on the history of North Dakota from the days of the dinosaurs to the present.

The *State Historical Society* (Bismarck) maintains numerous exhibits on the state's early history, Native American history, pioneer life, and natural history.

Universities and Colleges

In 2006, North Dakota had 13 public and eight private institutions of higher learning.

ANNUAL EVENTS

January–March

North Dakota Winter Show in Valley City (March)

North Dakota Horse Fest in Minot (March)

April–June

Fort Seward Wagon Train in Jamestown (June)

Fort Union Rendezvous near Williston (June)

Old Time Fiddlers Contest at the International Peace Garden (June)

Medora Musical in Medora (June through Labor Day)

July–September

Jaycee Rodeo Days in Mandan (early July)

Governor's Cup Walleye Fishing Tournament on Lake Sakakawea (July)

German Folk Festival in Fargo (July)

North Dakota State Fair in Minot (July)

Roughrider Days in Dickinson (July)

Champions Ride Rodeo in Sentinel Butte (August)

Pioneer Days at Bonanzaville, USA, in West Fargo (August)

Folkfest in Bismarck (mid-September)

Potato Bowl in Grand Forks (September)

United Tribes Powwow in Bismarck (September)

October–December

Norsk Høstfest in Minot (October)

Party in the Pumpkin Patch in Fargo (October)

Threshing Bee in Makoti (October)

Christmas on the Prairie at Bonanzaville, USA, in West Fargo (December)

Medora Musical

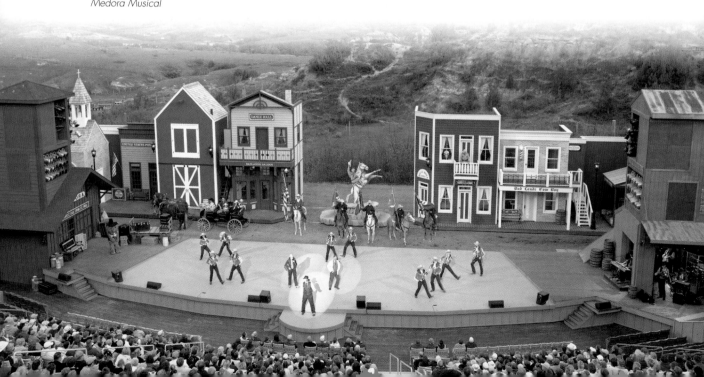

BIOGRAPHICAL DICTIONARY

Lynn Anderson (1947–) is a country music singer who rose to stardom with her 1970 hit single "(I Never Promised You a) Rose Garden." She was born in Grand Forks.

Maxwell Anderson (1888–1959) wrote many award-winning plays and screen adaptations, such as *Anne of the Thousand Days* and *All Quiet on the Western Front.* He spent his teenage and young adult years in Jamestown, Grand Forks, and Minnewaukan.

Robert H. Bahmer (1904–1990), who was born near Gardena, served as the archivist of the United States from 1966 to 1968.

Buffalo Bird Woman (1839?–1932) told the story of her own life and the ways of the Hidatsa people to writer Gilbert L. Wilson. He wrote two books filled with her observations.

Anne Carlsen (1915–2002), who was born missing both hands and feet, was an advocate for people with disabilities. After earning a doctorate, she became head of a school for disabled children in Jamestown, which was renamed the Anne Carlsen Center for Children.

Buffalo Bird Woman

Warren Christopher (1925–), a statesman born in Scranton, negotiated the release of American hostages from Iran in 1980, helped bring about a better relationship with China, and served as U.S. secretary of state from 1993 to 1997.

Shannon Curfman (1985–), a blues-rock guitarist and singer, had a hit album, *Loud Guitars, Big Suspicions*, when she was just 14 years old. She was born in Fargo.

Ronald N. Davies (1904–1996) grew up in Grand Forks and became a federal judge in Fargo. In 1957, he made worldwide headlines by ordering that Little Rock, Arkansas, educate black and white students in the same schools.

Marquis de Mores See page 108.

Angie Dickinson (1931–) is an actor who was born in Kulm. She has appeared in more than 30 movies, including *Rio Bravo*, the original *Ocean's Eleven* in 1960, and the 2001 remake of the same film. In the 1970s, she starred in the TV series *Police Woman*, playing the first strong woman character in a crime series.

Ivan Dmitri (1900–1968) was an artist and photographer. He was born Levon West and lived in many different North Dakota towns during his childhood.

Angie Dickinson

Josh Duhamel (1972–) is an actor who was born in Minot and has starred in the TV shows "All My Children" and "Las Vegas," as well as films such as *Transformers*.

Carl Ben Eielson (1897–1929), who was born in Hatton, was an aviation pioneer who flew the first airmail route in 1924 and co-piloted flights over the Arctic and Antarctica.

Laura J. Eisenhuth (1858–1937) was elected superintendent of public education in North Dakota in 1892, making her the first U.S. woman to hold statewide elected office.

Louise Erdrich See page 77.

Darin Erstad (1974–), of Jamestown, is a Major League Baseball player who has played for the Houston Astros, the Los Angeles Angels, and the Chicago White Sox.

John Bernard Flannagan (1895–1942), born in Fargo, was a sculptor known for his abstract figures of animals carved from stone.

Phyllis Frelich (1944–) is an actor who attended the School for the Deaf in her hometown of Devils Lake. She won a Tony Award for her performance in *Children of a Lesser God*, a play written for her. She also founded the National Theatre of the Deaf.

Josh Duhamel

Bertin C. Gamble See page 100.

William H. Gass (1924–), who was born in Fargo, is a noted fiction writer who experiments with words and punctuation.

Travis Hafner (1977–) is one of the best power hitters in Major League Baseball. He was born in Jamestown.

Phillip Allen Hansen (1968–), born in Ellendale, played defensive end for the Buffalo Bills football team.

Brynhild Haugland (1905–1998) served in the North Dakota House of Representatives for 52 years before she retired in 1990. No other state legislator in the United States served as long.

Phil Jackson See page 79.

Leon O. Jacobson (1911–1992) was a doctor, professor, and administrator who headed the University of Chicago's Department of Medicine and set up cancer research and treatment institutions. He was born in Sims.

Darin Erstad

David C. Jones (1921–), a career air force officer, served two terms as chairman of the Joint Chiefs of Staff of the U.S. Armed Forces from 1978 to 1982. Before that, he was chief of staff of the U.S. Air Force. He grew up in Minot.

Woody Keeble See page 64.

Cora Smith King (1867–1939) was a member of the first graduating class of the University of North Dakota in 1889, and in 1892 became the first woman licensed to practice medicine in North Dakota. She also worked for women's right to vote.

Jim Kleinsasser (1977–), who was born in Carrington, plays fullback and tight end for the Minnesota Vikings.

Louis L'Amour (1908–1988) was a writer who produced more than 400 novels, short stories, and screenplays during his career, most about the American West. He was born in Jamestown.

Pierre Gaultier de La Vérendrye See page 35.

Cora Smith King

Jonny Lang (1981–) is a blues singer whose albums include *Lie to Me*, *Wander This World*, and *Long Time Coming*. He was born in Fargo.

William "Wild Bill" Langer See page 62.

Peggy Lee See page 78.

William Lemke (1878–1950) was a progressive reformer and member of the Nonpartisan League who helped create the state-owned bank, grain elevator, and mill. He served as North Dakota's attorney general and served several terms in the U.S. House of Representatives. He grew up on a homestead in Towner County.

Roger Maris (1934–1985) grew up in Grand Forks and Fargo and became one of the greatest hitters in Major League Baseball. He belted 61 home runs in 1961, a record that lasted 37 years.

Gerald P. Nye See page 86.

Casper Oimoen (1906–1995) was a champion skier and ski jumper who also served as captain of the 1936 U.S. Olympic Ski Team. He was born in Norway but immigrated to North Dakota.

Jim Kleinsasser

Clifford "Fido" Purpur (1912–2001) in 1933 became the first North Dakotan to play in the National Hockey League. After retiring from hockey in 1947, he coached at the University of North Dakota.

Chester Reiten (1923–), the owner of a radio and television broadcasting company, founded Norsk Høstfest, the state's annual Scandinavian festival. He was born in Hastings.

Theodore Roosevelt See page 89.

James Rosenquist (1933–), who was born in Grand Forks, became a leading painter and printmaker in the pop art movement.

Sacagawea See page 39.

Harold Schafer (1912–2001), who was born near Stanton, founded the Gold Seal Company. The company made top-selling household products such as Mr. Bubble and Snowy Bleach. He loved the town of Medora and its history, and made Medora's restoration his lifelong work.

Eric Sevareid (1912–1992), who was born in Velva, was a journalist who made his name covering World War II and later became a pioneering television broadcaster on CBS.

Sitting Bull

Sitting Bull See page 53.

Ann Sothern (1909–2001), who was born Harriet Lake in Valley City, was a movie star in the 1930s and 1940s. In the 1950s and 1960s, she starred in two TV series, *Private Secretary* and *The Ann Sothern Show*.

Dorothy Stickney (1896–1998), born in Dickinson, was an actor who appeared in Broadway plays such as *Chicago* and *Life with Father*.

Era Bell Thompson See page 51.

Arthur C. Townley See page 59.

Bobby Vee (1943–) was a pop music star in the early 1960s, recording hits such as "Rubber Ball" and "The Night Has a Thousand Eyes." He was born in Fargo.

Lawrence Welk (1903–1992), born in Strasburg, was an accordion player and bandleader. His TV series, *The Lawrence Welk Show*, featured polkas, waltzes, and other music and aired from 1955 to 1982.

Larry Woiwode (1941–), who was born in Sykeston, is an award-winning novelist and the poet laureate of North Dakota. Several of his novels are set in North Dakota.

Eric Sevareid

RESOURCES

BOOKS

Nonfiction

Frazier, Neta Lohnes. *Path to the Pacific: The Story of Sacagawea*. New York: Sterling, 2007.

Garraty, John. *Teddy Roosevelt: American Rough Rider*. New York: Sterling, 2007.

Haugen, Brenda. *Crazy Horse: Sioux Warrior*. Mankato, MN: Compass Point, 2006.

Manning, Phillip. *Dinomummy*. Boston: Kingfisher, 2007.

Palazzo-Craig, Janet. *The Ojibwe of Michigan, Wisconsin, Minnesota, and North Dakota*. New York: PowerKids Press, 2005.

Patent, Dorothy Hinshaw. *The Buffalo and the Indians: A Shared Destiny*. Boston: Clarion Books, 2006.

Temple, Bob, and Teri Temple. *Welcome to Badlands National Park*. Mankato, MN: Child's World, 2006.

Webster, Christine. *The Lewis and Clark Expedition*. Danbury, CT: Children's Press, 2007.

Fiction

Blue Talk, Richard, and Jerome Fourstar. *How the Morning and Evening Stars Came to Be: And Other Assiniboine Indian Stories*. Helena: Montana Historical Society Press, 2003.

Calvert, Patricia. *Betrayed!* Topeka, KS: Rebound by Sagebrush, 2004.

Schultz, Jan Neubert. *Battle Cry*. Minneapolis: Carolrhoda Books, 2006.

Sneve, Virginia Driving Hawk. *Lana's Lakota Moons*. Lincoln, NE: Bison Books, 2007.

Spooner, Michael. *Last Child*. New York: Henry Holt, 2005.

DVDs

American Experience: TR: The Story of Theodore Roosevelt. PBS Paramount, 2006.

Biography—George Armstrong Custer: America's Golden Cavalier. A&E Home Video, 2006.

Biography—Sitting Bull: Chief of the Lakota Nation. A&E Home Video, 2005.

The Journey of Sacagawea. PBS Home Video, 2003.

National Geographic—Lewis & Clark: Great Journey West (Special Edition). National Geographic Video, 2004.

Save Our History—The Missouri: Journey with Stephen Ambrose. A&E Home Video, 2006.

WEB SITES AND ORGANIZATIONS

Kids Konnect—North Dakota

www.kidskonnect.com/content/view/198/27/

Find fast facts and links to more information about North Dakota.

North Dakota Parks and Recreation Department

www.ndparks.com

Find a state park, learn about bird-watching, or discover a scenic byway to drive down.

North Dakota Tourism

www.ndtourism.com

Find all kinds of fun facts about North Dakota, as well as places to go and things to do.

Northern Prairie Wildlife Research Center

www.npwrc.usgs.gov/resource/wetlands/basinwet/index.htm

A great place to learn about the wetlands of North Dakota and all the birds and other wildlife that live in them.

State Historical Society of North Dakota

www.nd.gov/hist

Find links to useful databases, historic preservation projects, exhibits, and other events, as well as a brief history of the state.

State of North Dakota

www.nd.gov

Learn about North Dakota's government.

INDEX

★ ★ ★

AUTHOR'S TIPS AND SOURCE NOTES

★ ★ ★

For research on the events that shaped the state, I found a wealth of information in a book with small type called *History of North Dakota* by Elwyn B. Robinson. The last edition of this wonderful book was published in 1995. Nevertheless, finding out about current events in the state is no problem, thanks to plenty of online sites. One Web site that was a pleasure to consult was the one maintained by the North Dakota Tourism Division (www.ndtourism.com). The site reflects the serious commitment the state has made to increasing its tourism industry. I had expected information on what to see and where to stay, but the site also has plenty to say about the state's history and economy. And it is full of fun facts that really are fun.

Photographs © 2010: age fotostock/Vic Bider: 21; akg-Images, London: 23 bottom, 122 top (Werner Forman), 23 top right, 24 top (Wilhelm Kuhnert); Alamy Images: 108 right, 114 bottom (Danita Delimont), 109 right (FAN travelstock), 33 bottom (Rolf Hicker Photography), 27 (Interfoto Pressebildagentur), 106 bottom (Andre Jenny), 111 left (Jason Lindsey); Courtesy of the American Museum of Natural History, Division of Anthropology: 4 bottom left, 76 (50.1/4363); AP Images: 130 center (Bill Haber), 82, 83 left, 87, 88, 90, 92, 100 right (Will Kincaid), 68, 96, 97 left, 124 (James MacPherson), 77 right (Dawn Villella); Art Resource, NY: 32 top, 33 top left (Albert Bierstadt/Harvard Art Museum), 32 bottom, 36 (Jean-Adolphe Bocquin/Bildarchiv Preussischer Kulturbesitz), 28 (George Catlin/Smithsonian American Art Museum, Washington, DC); Bridgeman Art Library International Ltd., London/New York: 44 bottom, 47, 53, 136 top (Robert Ottokar Lindneux/Private Collection/Peter Newark American Pictures); Chuck Haney: 10; Corbis Images: cover main (Tom Bean), 78, 79 bottom (Bettmann), back cover (Bloomimage), 97 right, 98 (Ron Chapple), 134 bottom (John Cordes/IconSMI), 15 (Najlah Feanny-Hicks), 46 (W.H. Illingworth/Bettmann), 70, 71 left (Karen Kent), 79 top (Jeff Lewis/Icon SMI), 58 (Minnesota Historical Society), 57 top right, 60 (Arthur Rothstein), 4 top right, 33 top right, 39 left (Smithsonian Institution); Daybreak Imagery/Richard Day: 4 top left, 9 right, 19, 120; Denver Public Library, Western History Collection/C.G. Morledge: 45 top right, 49 (X-31308); Everett Collection, Inc.: 43 (Seth Eastman), 42 (Mary Evans Picture Library), 57 bottom, 64 bottom (Rex USA), 62 (Wisconsin Historical Society), 86, 89, 136 bottom; Gary Alan Nelson: 8, 9 left; Getty Images: 134 top (James Devaney), 135 bottom (George Gojkovich), 133 top (Paul Harris); Institute for Regional Studies, NDSU Libraries, Fargo: 5 top right, 56 top, 57 top left (RS000635), 54 (RS003286); iStockphoto: 116 bottom, 130 bottom (Geoffrey Black), 130 top (David Freund), 45 bottom, 123 right (Hannamaria Photography), 128 (Vladislav Lebedinski); JupiterImages: 4 bottom right, 81 top, 99 (Brian Hagiwara), 81 bottom (Kevin Hewitt Photography); Courtesy of Katherine E. L'Amour and LouisLAmour.com: 77 left; Library and Archives Canada: 35; Library of Congress: 135 top; Minnesota Historical Society: 56 bottom, 59, 100 left, 133 bottom; Missouri Valley Historical Society/Marlette Pittman: 110 bottom; National Geographic Image Collection: 67 (Annie Griffiths Belt), 40 (W. Langdon Kihn); Courtesy of National Museum of the American Indian, Smithsonian Institution: 4 top center, 22 bottom, 25 (242955.000); North Dakota Tourism Department: 5 bottom, 71 right, 80, 106 top, 107 bottom, 109 left, 110 top, 111 right, 112, 113 bottom, 113 top, 114 top, 115 right, 115 left, 132; North Wind Picture Archives: 26; Ohio Historical Society/AL07213: 24 bottom; Paul Rezendes: 13; Perceptive Visions Stock Photography/Jason Lindsey: 107 top; Peter Arnold Inc./Jim Wark: 20; PhotoEdit/Don Smetzer: 39 right, 84; State Historical Society of North Dakota: 108 left (00042-106), 51 (0262-009), 48 (A4263), 44 top, 45 top left, 123 left (A4824), 63 (A6686-04), 50 (Joseph E. Pasonault/Williston State College Foundation/William E. Shemorry Photograph Collection); Superstock, Inc./George Catlin: 75; The Art Archive/Picture Desk/ Gianni Dagli Orti: 22 top, 23 top left (National Anthropological Museum, Mexico); The Granger Collection, New York: 30 (George Catlin), 5 top left, 52 (Frederic Remington), 37, 122 bottom; The Image Finders/Bill Leaman: 18; Tom Bean: 16, 129; Courtesy of U.S. Army Photo: 64 top; US Mint: cover inset, 116 top, 119; Vector-Images.com: 4 center, 83 right, 94, 95, 126, 127; VEER: 121 (Blend Images Photography), 74 (Digital Vision Photography).

Maps by Map Hero, Inc.